William Russell Dunham

Theory of medical science

The doctrine of an inherent power in medicine a fallacy

William Russell Dunham

Theory of medical science
The doctrine of an inherent power in medicine a fallacy

ISBN/EAN: 9783337041748

Printed in Europe, USA, Canada, Australia, Japan

Cover: Foto ©ninafisch / pixelio.de

More available books at **www.hansebooks.com**

THEORY OF MEDICAL SCIENCE.

THE DOCTRINE OF AN INHERENT POWER IN MEDICINE A FALLACY.

THE ULTIMATE SPECIAL PROPERTIES OF VITALITY AND THE LAWS OF VITAL FORCE CONSTITUTE THE FUNDAMENTAL BASIS OF MEDICAL PHILOSOPHY AND SCIENCE.

BY

WILLIAM R. DUNHAM, M. D.

"If we are weak, let us fall back upon tradition and belief for support; if we are strong, let us see what there is outside of belief, and don't care what the world says." — *Louis Agassiz.*

BOSTON:
JAMES CAMPBELL, PUBLISHER.
1876.

INTRODUCTION.

In the preparation of this volume, I have omitted many of the theoretical details belonging to the science, with the view only of pointing out our more important fallacies, and the recovery of the fundamental principles involved in a correct theory of medical science.

It is very important that the profession should have a reliable theory by which the problems of the science can be more satisfactorily explained, affording a better guide in the details of practice ; also that the non-professional should be sufficiently acquainted with the general principles of our profession to enable them to distinguish between quackery and rational practice.

I have endeavored to illustrate the principles in the most simple, brief, and effectual manner, and where it was possible, to avoid the use of technical terms above the comprehension of the average mind, and give a vividness to the idea without pretensions to elegance or literary merit.

CONTENTS.

PART FIRST.

CHAP.		PAGE
I.	SCIENCE	7
II.	FORCE AND ITS APPLICATION	15
III.	THEORY OF VITAL FORCE, OR VITALITY	23
IV.	THE APPLICATION OF THE THEORY OF VITALITY. — DISEASE	49
V.	MATERIA MEDICA	80

PART SECOND.

DIFFERENT SYSTEMS OF PRACTICE	105
THE PRESENT STATE OF MEDICAL PHILOSOPHY	117
THE DRIFT OF MEDICAL RESEARCH AND ITS INFLUENCE ON THE PEOPLE	126
CONCLUSION. — THE PLAN OF LIFE	135

SYNOPSIS.

The present basis of the theory of medical science is indoctrinated from TWO sources or powers, which are made responsible for the activities manifested by the human organisms in health and disease, namely, the presumed latent and inherent power in *materia medica* and *poisons*, and the inherent power of the organism or vital power.

The supposed power in *materia medica* and *poisons* is an error of gigantic magnitude, which has no place in nature, and is the greatest delusion of thought ever adopted by civilized humanity.

The science of medicine is based on only ONE source of power, namely, the VITAL POWER; and a correct theory of vitality demonstrates the ideal delusion which has invested *materia medica* and *poisons* with active principles or inherent powers.

The relation of *materia medica* and *poisons* to the human organism not one of *power*, but one of *cause*.

Causes may be derived from various sources, but organic activities in health and disease receive their momentum from vital power.

A REVOLUTION IN MEDICAL PHILOSOPHY IS INEVITABLE. No change suggested in the practice of our science, but a different explanation demanded.

The incorporated errors in the presumed first principles have proved very disastrous to the non-professional as well as the profession, and given improper direction to thought, thus abridging the utility to be derived from a correct knowledge of the science.

PART FIRST.

CHAPTER I.

SCIENCE.

A SCIENCE is not alone the assemblage of facts in nature: but includes a knowledge of the laws, which explain those facts in a rational manner. Facts are merely the elements of a science; but until those facts have been sifted and compared, and general principles or laws deduced therefrom, which correctly account for the successive order of incidents, we have no science.

The theory of a science consists in the explanation of those laws, on which facts are dependent; thus a science embraces not only facts, but the philosophy of how, and why they occur.

The three great natural sciences, namely, Astronomy, Chemistry, and Medicine, constitute the more primary and important branches which have engaged the attention of philosophers; to elucidate for practical purposes the laws which .govern each department. Astronomy and chemistry, after struggling through a long period of discordant philosophies, finally triumphed by the recovery of those principles or laws which afford a correct explanation of the facts in their respective departments; and are consequently called the positive sciences.

To enumerate the various theories which have been put forward, to explain the phenomena of astronomical facts, and their strong hold on the belief of the people, which have now passed into oblivion — or the various doctrines of Alchemy, out of which chemistry became developed to a science — would avail nothing except to illustrate how ardently the people have grasped those errors, and sought their perpetuation; also their great reluctance to yield them up and give place to principles which now guide all students of those departments, through similar channels of thought.

The doctrines to-day of the sciences of astronomy and chemistry are based on a correct recognition of the law; consequently there is but one school of philosophy which indoctrinates theories, in explanation of the general facts involved in those sciences, and we are thus persuaded to admit, that a science whose primary principles are correctly interpreted, furnishes but one system or school of philosophy.

So long as the facts of a science are not explainable on recognized primary principles, which are both *probable* and *incontrovertible*, there will be a variety of schools each laboring to gain numerous converts to their particular belief. We may thus with propriety, in view of our present condition, ask if the medical doctrines of the various schools are entitled to be classified as correct principles of a science? It is generally conceded that the science of medicine is already established. We certainly have a large assemblage of positive facts, but not, however, until those facts can be explained on one set of principles, can we claim to be indoctrinating the principles or correct theory of science.

A careful survey of the various theories and systems of medical practice which contribute to make up the professions of the age, each earnestly advocated with a zeal untiring and worthy of all praise, contrasts most strangely with the idea that our Creator provided but one code of laws, which govern health and account for the phenomena of disease. Also, that He provided but one code which is involved in a correct explanation of vital force, and the relation of *materia medica* to the human system.

Some of the errors of our theories to-day may be difficult and slow to reason into oblivion, notwithstanding they have no true ideal in nature; but are entailed upon our belief, with such an honesty of purpose, that to oppose, seems like offending proprieties. Thus for a long time, generations have come into the world philosophically weighted with a destiny against which they have had no power to contend.

With this realizing sense of our situation it is not difficult, however, to reason up to a point of agreement with those of *our* school, that the others are very much in the wrong; but each school of theory is inclined to refuse to be reasoned against; and the different schools of medicine have each settled down into a state of self-consciousness that they are the wise ones, the true disciples of nature.

"It is not difficult to satisfy intelligent men that there is a design in nature; but the problem consists in becoming able to recognize what that design is."

With the numerous dissimilar theories and systems on

one side, and the belief that there was a design on the other, the inference certainly follows that there is an error in some school of philosophy; that there must be incorporated into the doctrines of science principles which are erroneous; yet to multitudes of earnest and intelligent people, each school has much the appearance of truth. Each school denies harboring the monster Error, but they can see the form, wandering through the halls of rival institutions.

If there is any science in our profession, the legitimate duty of inquiry and research consists in recovering the original ideas, and pursuing them correctly through their various intricate windings, enabling us to recognize the primary principles with a correctness so self-evident, that all who study the science unavoidably arrive at the same conclusion. The present idea on the part of the different schools is, in substance, that they are in possession of nearly all the great fundamental principles of the science; out of which they have constructed numerous theories for the elucidation of the facts, and that the admitted problems, yet unsolved, are not enigmas through any mistake which has been already made, but are such in consequence of some unrecognized principle, which is desirable to discover and *add* to our present basis for theoretical use. I shall, however, claim the reverse, that those enigmas have an existence in consequence of an error, which we have already perpetrated, in the recognition of principles.

The classification of the principles of a science are not of human contrivance, but are the recovery of those ideas that were in the Creative mind. And to better illustrate our situation by analogy, I will refer to the science of astronomy. During the early study of this science mankind reasoned from appearances, and the sun was supposed to revolve around our earth; theories were constructed to account for the position of planets by cycles and epicycles, until it required five circular motions to explain the irregularities of a single planet. Theorizing from this basis, complexities multiplied until the celebrated King Alphonso remarked that "if he had been consulted at the creation he could have done the thing better."

It is generally admitted that the following rule holds good under all circumstances: That when pursuing the study of a science and a principle is recognized, out of which there is to be developed the details of a science, should that principle be erroneous, the further it is pursued the greater the complexities, which require multiplied inventions to overcome; and thus discordant and contradictory theories will sooner or later make philosophers exclaim like Alphonso. Reversely, if a true principle is recognized, the further the subject is pursued, the more we admire the harmony and see the wisdom of the Creative mind. We readily understand that the science of astronomy, studied from its early recognized basis, was no science; the facts were established, but the principle or theory was erroneous. Therefore, the phenomena remained a mystery, because the people were in possession of no law by which to explain them.

Eventually the mind became more comprehensive, and it was necessary to surrender those early views or interpretations; but it was very humiliating to philosophic pride to thus yield that position, even untenable as it now appears; and history informs us that attempts to make this change were received with much reluctance; which illustrates not only the tenacity, but the almost utter impossibility for mankind to comprehend principles in opposition to long continued customs.

When they changed their base and pursued the investigation with the idea that the sun was the central body, and recognizing the law or force of gravitation as the immediate controlling force, mankind recovered those primitive ideas of the design, and thus developed correctly the details of a science out of which is now a harmonious whole, embodying principles which are unfolded alike to all intelligent humanity.

How is it with medical science? Are we entangled, like ancient astronomers, with erroneous first principles? Have we interpreted a principle out of which we are endeavoring to develop the details of a science, and have yet to learn that it is false? Must we surrender some of those principles which have ever been the base of our medical philosophy? These are questions for our consideration.

Are we, in this age of wisdom, — an age endowed with more intelligence than we have reason to believe ever existed in the human family previous to our time, — the victims of antiquated errors, errors which have been transmitted by those who have ever been the shining lights, to guide us from time immemorial to the present era? Such are the thoughts to be presented in the following pages.

Are you ready to consider it? Are you a devout and

sincere disciple of Science, willing to surrender those conventional principles which contribute to the present pomp and pride of medical lore, and accept a new basis for Science' sake? Remember that mankind, the most exalted production of God's creative power, must necessarily be enveloped with the surrounding of laws more intricate and difficult to interpret, than relate to those inanimate orbs of the solar system; yet contemporaneous with that period when man contemplated the wonders of the universe and sought to recover the primitive idea, out of which to develop the sciences — at the very period when his imagination interpreted the earth as the centre of the solar system, his imagination also established a principle to explain the facts of medical science.

At this time, reasoning from appearances only, man established primary principles for both sciences. The one relating to astronomy was very insignificant compared with the other, yet it deluded the mind of man for centuries; but was finally proved to be false. The other, relating to medical science, has continued to be transmitted to our generation, and it is my purpose to convince the reader that that principle is also false. Reasoning by analogy: if at that time the brain power was not sufficient to cope with the lesser problem, an opinion from the same source relating to a more profound one should be received under protest.

The imaginative principle to which I refer, anciently established, which is indoctrinated by our schools to-day, is that which endows *materia medica and poisons* with *inherent powers* that can *act* on the human organism.

I now assert that this accepted principle is a fallacy;

and I shall establish incontrovertible premises in support of this assertion in the following pages. The immutability of God's plan when revealed to us, constitutes the principle of a science ; and is not in harmony with that fixedness of purpose when it interprets the activity manifested in living tissue, as being dependent on *powers*, endowed *both* to organic and inorganic matter ; such interpretation would not be in harmony with the doctrine of Special Laws, and would invalidate the claim which provides for the existence of a science ; which implies that each department in nature is fulfilled by an activity ordained in a special law of force.

CHAPTER II.

FORCE AND ITS APPLICATION.

THE term force is employed to designate a power which moves matter and produces change. Matter and force are inseparable; thus we know nothing of force, except through matter. Our solar system has, inherent to its various orbs, a force or power which keeps them in constant motion; we know nothing of the power isolated from the material; yet through the material, we become aware not only of its existence, but acquire a knowledge of its laws; and can predict the time at which certain astronomical events will take place. We call this force the power of gravitation — this force keeps in motion our planetary system, with an unerring certainty, acting on all bodies, at all distances; and a knowledge of this law enables this department to become one of the positive sciences. All matter is susceptible to the force of gravitation; and various divisions and subdivisions of matter are susceptible to other superadded special forces. Chemical force is like the force of gravitation in one respect; that is, it acts on all matter, but unlike it in another respect, it acts only at *insensible distances*, while gravitation acts at all distances. Chemical force acts to produce those changes of matter, which enter into combinations, thus producing a substance unlike either of the separate elements which form the compound.

Water is a compound body composed of oxygen and hydrogen, whose separate elements in their ultimate state are gases; chemical force is expressed oftentimes as the law of affinity; that is, certain elements are said to have an affinity for each other, when they enter into combination. Among the sub-forces involved in chemical operations, may be mentioned cohesive force, which holds particles of the same kind together, as lead, silver, and gold. Heat force separates these particles; thus antagonizing the force of cohesion. The whole material universe, mineral, vegetable, and animal, when reduced to an ultimate analysis, consists of only about sixty-five elements, or different kinds of matter. And the different ways which this matter is combined by the various forces, gives variety to the mineral, vegetable, and animal world.

These sixty-five elements which comprise all this material world, are divided into two grand divisions, for purposes of study; the line of separation is made by a limited ability of certain forces. Thus chemical force acts *on all* these elements to form chemical compounds; while organic forces act on only about sixteen of the elements to form organic compounds or bodies. Thus, all those elements which are used by the organic forces, vegetable and animal, are called organic elements; and those which the organic forces will not use, are called inorganic elements. Thus we study the material as related to the organic and inorganic forces. Chemical force is an inorganic force; the products not being possessed of life. Organic forces are again sub-divided into two grand divisions, namely, vegetable forces, and animal forces, each of which has a great variety of special sub-divisions manifested in the different species of vegetable and animal life.

Vegetable forces organize material, and form certain bodies; and chemical force disorganizes that material, and takes the body to pieces. Thus, chemical force antagonizes vegetable force; one builds organisms, and the other destroys them. Also animal forces build organisms, and chemical force tears them asunder; thus chemical force takes both vegetable and animal organisms back to their elementary condition. Another distinction in regard to the organic forces, consists in the different abilities of the vegetable force and animal force, in the obtaining of material for their separate organizations.

Vegetable force has the ability to take the *elements*, and *chemical compounds*, to form organisms, and draw its support from this source only.

Animal force cannot take the elements, or chemical compounds, and appropriate and assimilate them as constituents of an animal organism, but all animal bodies have to obtain their support from the vegetable organisms.

All animal life, from the lowest to the highest, draws its nourishment, directly or indirectly, from vegetable products; thus the vegetable is a development between the mineral and animal.

No animal organism can assimilate any material as nutriment, except it has been previously subjected to the changes wrought by vegetable force; one animal, like the carnivorous or the fishes of the sea, may eat and assimilate the material of another animal; but this same material has at some previous period been subjected to the forces of vegetation, and been thus previously organized. This law holds good in every instance; consequently chemical compounds prepared by nature or by art are never within the reach of vital powers, and cannot be digested or assimilated by animal forces.

It is well to remember this distinction, for there are certain medical theories in regard to iron and other elements which, chemically prepared, are urged upon the belief of the public as chemical food; the error of these theories is apparent, when we consider that the foregoing laws are never suspended.

Water, a chemical compound, forms a constituent part of the animal organism; but it is not digested or assimilated, as we understand the term. It remains water, and is unchanged, becoming the vehicle by which nutrient material is conveyed to the blood, and through the blood to all parts of the system; also the only vehicle through which waste or effete matter is conveyed from all parts of the system to the excretory organs for removal.

Atmospheric air, containing oxygen in its elementary state, fulfills an important duty in the animal organism; but it is not assimilated like the constituent oxygen of a vegetable product, but fulfills a chemical relation, favoring elimination and regulating temperature; thus respiration employs physical principles for physiological purposes.

The relation of chemical force to the formation of animal organisms, consists in inducing changes in matter, within the organism, which more readily renders the waste material susceptible of elimination. When vitalized matter has fulfilled its usefulness to the organism, and vital force has ceased to use it, chemical force may induce changes which favor its escape. Also, chemical force may induce changes within the body, forming products which are the cause of disease; and again the causes of disease may be rendered less obnoxious by chemical change and more easily eliminated.

Chemical force will develop heat, also animal force will develop heat, and just what proportion of animal heat is due to chemical force, may be difficult to determine.

All vegetative products are not food for the human species, but it is very probable that each individual vegetation may produce a product, susceptible of becoming assimilated by the organism of some animal species.

Those vegetable products we recognize as food when deprived of their own vital functions may become constituents of a higher organization, that is, constituents of animal organisms; but cannot become food for other plants without being subjected to the retrograde changes induced by chemical force.

The animal organism, after being deprived of life, can be transformed into other animal organisms, but cannot be transformed into a vegetable organism, without first being returned by chemical agency to the elementary state.

When thus returned, vegetable force reconstructs the same materials; but its own protoplasm cannot be transformed from vegetable to vegetable. Vegetable protoplasm can be transformed to animal protoplasm, and when thus organized, animal protoplasm can be transformed to other animal protoplasm, indefinitely.

The inference might be that the further we continued the transfer of animal protoplasm, the less enduring would be animal life thus nourished.

Protoplasm signifies matter endowed with life so organized that it performs organic function; the same matter deprived of life but not disorganized is also a protoplasm until it has undergone decomposition. Animal organisms cannot make protoplasm from ultimate elements, but must take them from plants or some other animal. Therefore, for the origin of protoplasm, we must depend on the vegetable world: plants are the accumulators and animals the distributors.

These conditions of transfers, seem to be one way designed for the preservation of human life; even if it is not the best way, it would be preferable under certain circumstances, and illustrates the admirable wisdom of our Creator, by affording means for preserving and prolonging our existence. The idea is a grand one. The vegetable is not functionally self supporting, but self producing; while animal organisms are both self supporting and self producing. Man may transfer the vegetable protoplasm into his own organization, or certain herbivorous animals may transfer a vegetable protoplasm from those kinds of vegetation which man cannot transfer, and this protoplasm can be transferred for our use; also the herbivorous animal may be eaten by another animal, and this one by another, and so continue; and man at any period of these transfers can appropriate the protoplasm for his own support, thus affording testimony that even our worldly life is cared for in a manner unlike any other species.

There is something beautiful in the association of thought, that the force of gravitation prepares the way for chemical force, chemical force prepares the way for vegetable force, and vegetable force prepares the way for animal force, and animal force prepares the way for a higher order of force called human or brain force, possessed of mental faculties which enable us to look back upon the succession of changes upon which humanity is dependent, and take into comprehension a similitude of thought, and recover the original idea of design.

It is maintained by some scientists that force is a unit variously manifested. Now, even admitting that to be so, it is not within our limits to recognize it as such; we can only become familiar with its expression and laws as manifested in the several departments of science.

There is a law and order to each special department, and when we understand what that law and order is, we have fulfilled the very extent of our research in that particular direction.

During the early study of science, more importance was attached to the peculiarities of physical phenomena, than the inquiry into the basis or law of force on which the phenomena was dependent. The theory of an unseen force has been considered as tending more to make a visionary student than a practical man, consequently the theory of the law of force has always advanced in the background. It is only after a long period of philosophical grievance that theory becomes capable of maintaining a dignity which courts respect and which establishes permanent modes of thinking.

The rational explanation of all phenomena implies

the necessity of a theory of force. A theory may have a superstructure built on imagination alone, or it may have material facts for an attainable opinion, surrounded by firm frontiers of reason and coöperative judgment; and such a one affords a mighty instrument for defining ideas into practical shape.

All science is based on some power or force which is responsible by its laws for the course events take; and it becomes important to inquire where that power or force resides which is involved in the science of medicine, and what are its laws and in what it is inherent.

CHAPTER III.

THEORY OF VITAL FORCE OR VITALITY.

ORGANIC forces, both vegetable and animal, are called vital forces; and the vital force or vitality is the sum of the energies of a living body. It is that principle or power which establishes our individuality, and is a distinct force that converts certain material into vitalized or living tissues executing those duties called physiological functions, and is also endowed with a limited ability of self-preservation.

We are not to consider this power as an entity, for such is beyond the limit of mental research; but ascertain how this power expresses itself in our organism or individuality; that is, learn whether it manifests itself merely by one peculiar property, or several distinct properties.

The force of gravitation has but one property or way of manifesting itself, which is the tendency to draw all bodies to one common centre. Each planetary body having this power, enables the different orbs to overcome opposing attractions, and maintain their relative position and path through the immensity of space.

The human organism is a more complex body, and is endowed not only with the distinct force, vitality; but this force has *distinct properties*, or ways of manifesting itself, and what *each* of those ultimate properties fulfill, as an expression of vital power, becomes the extreme limit of our research. We cannot go behind that law of manifestation and comprehend anything more remote. In order to take our position in the scale of development it becomes important to notice that stones grow; plants grow and live; animals grow, live, and have motion, sensation, and sensibility.

The peculiar, distinct, ultimate vital properties, which in the aggregate include all there is of vital force, are made apparent to our senses through the three properties of CONTRACTILITY, SENSATION, and SENSIBILITY.

Those three vital properties, or distinct ways of manifesting life force, are all there is involved in our individualization, and relate us to ourselves and the external world.

Every motion, function, or action manifested in the human system which is an evidence of life, is dependent on one or more of these three vital properties. We cannot go behind them more remotely, but can advance from this basis and recognize complexities of organic function and action. Therefore, in order to acquire a correct theory of vitality or knowledge of the laws through which this force is manifested, it is important to recognize all that each one of these vital properties can do, as an expression of that principle we call vitality.

CONTRACTILITY is that vital property which executes motion or movement; it alone executes every action we call a motion, through a certain class of nerves, and this class of nerves never do anything but this one function, and are called the nerves of motion.

The elevation of the papillæ of the skin, which are called " goose pimples," and the contraction of muscular fibres in all parts of the body, the executing of the heart's movements, the motions in respiration, are each a manifestation of this principle.

Contractility is manifested only by muscular fibre; and two unlike and distinct sources generate a power which gives momentum or activity to this property, and occasions it to execute motion; namely, instinct, and intellect or will.

The motions of organic life, such as the heart's action and respiration, and all those functions pertaining to organic development, are presided over by an instinct which is generated in the ganglionic centres. Voluntary motions are presided over by the will which is generated by the brain.

The instinct may generate a power, and give momentum to convulsive actions in those muscles usually under the control of the will. And again, certain muscles which are not under the control of the will, like the muscles of the heart, may have their rhythmical action suspended by a spasmodic action, and death ensue; thus illustrating that action, authorized by the instinct, is not always rhythmical and innocent.

How instinct or will is generated, is beyond our limit of research; the fact alone that it is generated and the laws by which it is manifested, includes all that is possible for us to know.

Instinct and will, both authorize activities through that vital property, contractility; thus the ganglionic centres and the brain, have the ability to give direction to motion, and it is what these two guiding influences occasion to be done, that enables us to know that there is such a directing quality inherent to organization.

Instinct is a controlling organic attainment, generated by the ganglionic centres and cerebellum, or lower portion of the brain substance. Will is a controlling influence generated by the cerebrum or superior portion of the brain.

SENSATION is that vital property which recognizes contact, either on the surface or inside among the structures; those nerves which recognize contact or touch fulfill no other duty. Sensation is performed at insensible distances, and it may be pleasant and agreeable or irritable to various degrees of pain; it is, nevertheless, a sensation.

Whatever the sensation may be is conveyed to the ganglionic centres, and may be conveyed to the brain; thus sensations are conveyed to two unlike sources of generated powers: one the ganglionic centre and cerebellum, where instinct is generated, and the other the cerebrum, where the will is generated. Ganglionic centres are distributed all over the organism, and consist of a small mass of nerve-like substance, from which more or less nerve fibres lead and connect with other similar centres, also lead to the various muscles which are to receive the impulse of motion. Nerves of sensation and nerves of motion both lead to the ganglionic centres, and from these ganglionic centres, nerves not only lead to other similar centres, but also communicate with the spinal cord, and thence to the brain; all of which complex operations are of much importance, but unnecessary to mention, in the fulfillment of my purpose.

Says Brown-Sequard: "If we separate a nervous centre from the nerves we find that in four days the nerve has lost its power altogether. It seems, therefore, that something came from the nervous centre which was useful in the production of forces there."

Sensations conveyed to a nerve centre, or sensory ganglion like the cerebellum, occasion a diction through instinct, manifested in the property of contractility or motion. Sensations conveyed to the brain or cerebrum may occasion a diction through the agency of the will, manifested by the property of motion or contractility.

Certain sensations may be conveyed to the nerve centres, and not to the cerebrum or brain; that is, those which are in relation to harmonious duties, to be performed by instinct, as assimilation and heart's action, and various other functions; but all sensations which are conveyed to the brain, are conveyed also to the nerve centre. Thus, the instinct may be sufficient to fulfill the required duty, but, if necessary, the brain may afford aid.

Respiration may be carried on through either influence; the sensations by the pneumogastric nerves are conveyed to the respiratory ganglion, or nerve centre, and instinct exert its influence through the phrenic nerve and gives motion to the diaphragm. Or the sensation may be carried to the medulla-oblongata and receive an impulse from the brain, which can give motion to the diaphragm.

With a view to illustrate the indistinctness of thought, which pervades the minds of eminent scientific philosophers, I quote from an address, delivered by Prof. T. H. Huxley, before the British Scientific Association. In alluding to the functions of the brain, he remarks:—

"The first proposition that you find definitely and clearly stated by Descartes is one which will sound very familiar to you at the present day.

"It is the view, which he was the first, so far as I know, to state not only definitely but upon sufficient grounds, that the brain is the organ of sensation, of thought, and of emotion, — that certain changes which take place in the matter of the brain are the essential antecedents of those states of consciousness which we term sensation, thought, and emotion. . . . . If it should happen to a man that by accident his spinal cord is broken across, he becomes paralyzed below the point of injury. In such a case his limbs would be absolutely paralyzed; he would have no control over them, and they would be entirely insensible. You might prick his feet or burn them, or do anything else you like with them, and they would be absolutely insensible. Consciousness, therefore, so far as we can have any knowlege of it, is entirely abolished in that part of the central nervous apparatus which lies below the injury. . . . . He is not paralyzed, in the sense of their being deprived of motion, for if you tickle the soles of his feet with a feather the limbs will be drawn up just as vigorously, perhaps a little more vigorously, than when he was in full possession of the consciousness of what happened to him."

Professor Huxley makes no distinction between sensation and sensibility, and makes thought and emotion factors of sensation, using consciousness and sensation as synonymous. He also ascribes sensibility and consciousness to the lower extremities. So long as we permit such an incongruous application of language, to describe

THEORY OF VITAL FORCE OR VITALITY. 29

two unlike vital properties, as if the two were one, we shall fail to comprehend the true theory of vitality.

Various degrees of pain and irritability as well as normal sensations, are included in that manifestion called sensation.

Thought, emotion, and consciousness are factors of sensibility.

Nothing can be more fatal to a correct knowledge of vitality than the omission to recognize the difference between organic sense or sensation, and intellectual sense or sensibility.

SENSIBILITY is that property or vital power manifested through the brain; different from sensation, which perceives only by instinct at insensible distances; while sensibility perceives at all distances, and generates that influence which directs voluntary motion. Thus, through these two properties of nerve perception we are made aware of things both near and distant; therefore, instinct and will, give direction to all motion manifested by the human organism. By sensibility " we trace the footsteps of our wise and intelligent architect throughout all this stupendous fabric."

The terms sensation and sensibility are used very promiscuously both by medical writers and lexicographers; in medical literature the term sensibility is often applied to express acute pain in local injuries; and lexicographers use it in the place of sensation, " as a frozen limb loses its sensibility." Such a promiscuous use of special terms is suicidal to positive science, and is not allowed in chemistry or astronomy.

Organic sense or sensation, is the sense of perception

by contact at insensible distances. Intellectual sense, or sensibility, is the sense of perception through the brain at all distances.

These three vital properties, briefly described, constitute the aggregate of all the vital forces; and how each behaves under all circumstances, comprises the details of applied vital force and theory of vital law. These three vital properties relate us to motion, to a knowledge of contact or touch, and the immensity of space. This is all there is of us; or in other words, all there is of us is manifested through these three vital properties.

Closely allied to these ultimate vital properties, we have the phenomena of irritability and reaction, or reflex action, which become very important phenomena, to be elucidated.

What is irritability? Our medical lexicon defines it, "A power, possessed by all living organized bodies, of being acted upon by certain stimuli, and moving responsive to stimulation. It is the ultimate vital property." If this definition is correct, and irritability is an ultimate vital property, we have four, instead of three ultimate vital properties. I pronounce this definition erroneous, and assert that it is not a "power acted upon by stimuli," but it is, however, a "power moving responsive to stimulation." There is a vast difference between the two statements.

The first, that it is a "power acted upon by stimuli," is equivalent to acknowledging that a stimulus is possessed of a power inherent to itself; which is one of the great fallacies I propose to disprove. That irritability is a "power moving responsive to stimulation," is not only

THEORY OF VITAL FORCE OR VITALITY.

correct, but requires a more detailed explanation. A correct understanding of the premises involved in this problem is of great value, not for this problem alone, but for the prevention of greater errors in the future.

To illustrate, we have, as factors of this problem, 1st, a nerve of motion; 2d, a nerve of sensation; 3d, the stimulus. The stimulus is brought in contact with the nerve of sensation. What does the stimulus do? Not anything, no more than a piece of bread would do in the stomach, so far as any inherent power is concerned. The nerves of sensation recognize the presence of the bread, and the organic instincts or inherent powers of the organisms act in a manner relative to its relation, and the required wants of the system. The same class of nerves recognize the presence of stimuli, and the organic instinct acts in a manner relative to its relation to the system. There is no inherent power in the bread, although it is used by the vital power in the functions of life. There is no inherent power in the stimulus, but stimuli afford a *cause* for a changed vital action, and becomes useful to the physician in directing the action of vital power. Thus, that part of the definition which implies that irritability is a "power possessed by all living bodies of being acted upon by certain stimuli," is erroneous.

But that irritability is a "power moving responsive to stimulation," is illustrated as follows: The stimulus applied to the nerve of sensation becomes a *cause*. The recognition of the stimulus by the nerve is *not action* of the stimulus; the nerve of sensation is not acted upon by any power, but the nerve, as an ultimate property of vital power, recognizes the presence of the stimulus, which is all the nerve does; and a knowledge of this presence is conveyed to the ganglionic centres, the generators of that power we call instinct; and this instinct gives direction to the nerves of motion, which occasion, perhaps, an acceleration of blood to the part if the stimulus was local.

This increase of blood gives redness, heat, and perhaps more fullness to the part, according to the amount of the cause, all things being equal. The parts thus changed are said to be in a state of irritability; that is, a disagreeable sensation may exist from the degree of congestion and heat which is now in contact with those nerves of sensation. The irritability consists only of an augmented or disagreeable sensation of the nerves in the particular region. The stimulus was the *irritant* or *cause*, not by virtue of a power inherent to the stimulus, but by its presence in contact with the nerves of sensation.

This explanation of the phenomena of irritability, through the three factors mentioned, furnishes the proof that the definition is erroneous in another respect, which is that irritability is not an " ultimate vital property." Irritability is not a vital property unlike sensation; it is sensation disagreeably augmented, nothing more or less. It is secondary, instead of being primary or ultimate; it is dependent on conditions supplied to the nerves of sensation, and is abnormal, consequently cannot be an ultimate vital property.

What is Reflex Action? It is a problem embracing the same factors included in irritability, namely, the nerves of motion, the nerves of sensation, and the stimulus, or cause, whatever it may be. The term " reflex action " implies that there has been a previous action. Let us search for the previous or primary action, and see of what it consists. The stimulus, or material cause, is applied to the nerve of sensation; sensation is not an action, and it is not in any way synonymous with action; sensation is sensation or knowledge of contact, and no other term can express it. The presence of the stimulus or material is recognized by the nerve of sensation, and the instinct, residing in the ganglionic centre, gives impulse to an action through the nerves of motion.

If sensation could be called an action, this impulse through the nerves of motion would be a secondary action, or reflex action; but the stimulus does nothing, it does not act, it is merely in contact with the nerve of sensation, and affords a different sensation only, which occasions all the thus caused action there is in the case; and this action is a primal or direct action, not a secondary or reflex action. This term, *reflex action*, is permitted, through expression, to support an incorrect idea.

The medical school philosophy is, that the stimuli acts on the nerve of sensation, and an action directed back, without the intervention of consciousness, takes place, and is denominated reflex action. If medical men persist in the use of the term, it is important that the idea so long associated with the stimulus, as having a power inherent to itself, which acts, should be discontinued. It seems to me, however, that the term *reflex operation* would be more appropriate, and better expressive of the occurrence.

The term *reflex action*, when applied to the human subject, seems either out of place or discordant with itself, for the plan on which we are designed, embraced in the ultimate expression of the three vital properties, — contractility, or motion; sensation; and sensibility, — permits the following illustration, of like applicability in principles, yet unlike in representation. When a stimulus is applied to the nerve of sensation, and that sensation is communicated only to the ganglionic centre, where instinct, without the intervention of consciousness, gives impulse to the motion, which increases the circulation of the part, or occasions spasmodic action of the muscles, like strychnia, we are instructed to call it reflex action.

But if the knowledge of the stimulus, which is applied to the nerve of sensation, is communicated to the brain, and the will, instead of the instinct, gives volition to a muscle, we call it direct action.

It seems equally proper to call both actions direct. The impulse given to one is generated in the ganglionic centre, while the other is generated in the brain, the applied cause and principle being alike. It is quite apparent that the term "reflex action" is an outgrowth through the belief that there was a primal action on the part of the stimulus, and on the same principle we might with the same propriety call digestion and respiration a reflex action; and say the food acted on the nerves of sensation, to which a responsive impulse reflected back that action, which elaborated the fluids for digestive purposes, or that the effete matter in the venous blood acted on the nerve of sensation, which was reflected back by the impulse of the pneumogastric ganglion, executing the muscular action of respiration, or reflex action.

I hope to make plain to the reader, before I complete

this volume, that the relation which we maintain to the material world is ordained on the plan that all the action on the part of, or expressed by, the living tissue, is a primary vital action. Our relation to the material of the universe and the immensity of space becomes known to us through the ultimate properties of *sensation* and *sensibility*, at insensible and sensible distances, and all action expressed by living tissues, receives its impulse, generated either in the nerve ganglions, called instinct, or in the brain, called will.

And whatever action is thus manifested, is in harmony with the relation which the said material maintains to the human organism, either usable or non-usable.

If too excessive, some of the usable material is expelled unused; and again, if the material is of that kind which is never used or assimilable, the generated impulse expresses a kind of action which has in view the elimination of the material sooner or later. This constitutes the aggregate, except the repair of mechanical injuries, aside from physiological duties, of that power called self-preservative, peculiar to organic life, generated and urged to activity; which superintends the physiological functions, selecting and appropriating that material which is usable; also rejecting that material which is not usable.

The three ultimate vital properties which make up the aggregate of all there is of power in a human organism, perform all those duties which living tissues can perform and express our whole relation to the material world and the universe at large. This plan reveals to us that vital power is the only power which gives momentum to vitalize tissue; that the doctrine of a power in medicine, which acts on our living tissues, seems to have no abiding place in the ordained plans of the human institution. Should I succeed in convincing the reader that medicine has *no power*, do not adopt the conclusion that it is of no use. Although looking at this subject from its present philosophical basis, and adopted belief, it would seem that if we should deprive it of a *power* it would be useless; but bear in mind, however, that its usefulness does not depend on the truth of the philosophy which our schools associate with it. The philosophy is only an invention, to explain a fact, but is not equal to the task. When we are convinced that medicine has no power, it does not change its relation of usefulness, but the law which expresses its usefulness must be explained on a different principle from that of an inherent power.

A human being is an organized product due to a certain ordained law of power, entitled vital force or vital power; and this vital power has its peculiar and distinctive manner of manifestation in a variety of ultimate and sub-properties, and its only object is, to develop, maintain, and protect the human organism, and every impulse generated by the ganglionic nerve centres, denominated instinct, are with a view to fulfill this only ordained purpose.

The action thus generated may appear wise or unwise, and it may be practically either. Our *sensibility* should acquire that culture and discernment which comprehends the tendency of the power manifested, and perceive whether this instinct is giving the best impulse to activity, in degree and kind, which the desired expectations of the case seem to justify; which may require only to be let alone; or perceive how much out of harmony with desired, expectant result; and guide and direct it; thus, with the knowledge of how it behaves under all circumstances, supply that kind and quantity of medicine which will, by virtue of its presence (not its power) occasion an action more in harmony with the best interests of the patient.

When God ordained man, He decreed him all the power that was necessary for him; He did not leave the supply of power to be furnished by the intellect, but created him in full possession of all necessary powers, with an intellectual ability to comprehend the law of those powers, and, to a limited extent, control the manifestations, by supplying the causes or material which would occasion this power to manifest itself to the best interests of the individual.

In connection with this plan of ordained power manifested involuntarily, we must necessarily recognize that the instinct, which presides more primarily over our organism, executes all those actions called physiological and pathological.

Physiological actions perform those duties pertaining to nutrition and assimilation, maintaining that balance of function termed health, while pathological action involves those duties or actions pertaining to things not usable for assimilative purposes, which must, sooner or later, become eliminated for the preservation of the individual,— thus, healthy anatomy is the result of physiological action, and morbid anatomy the result of pathological action, both kinds of action receiving the necessary impulse from the source denominated instinct.

LAWS OF VITAL POWER.

The special ultimate vital properties are governed primarily by certain laws, which we will notice in the following order : —

THE FIRST LAW of vital force, with a view to self-preservation, executes the required physiological duties, and is the subject taught in the name of physiology.

THE SECOND LAW of vital force, with a view to self-preservation, executes the pathological actions, that is, all actions which are in relation to material, not for physiological purposes, and is the subject erroneously taught, as the *action* of a *power* inherent to poison, and in the cause of disease, and inherent to medicine.

The second class or law of actions, in relation to poisons and the cause of disease, we will again subdivide into two divisions.

First, Pathological actions which require to be understood, but not medicated, because they are doing the best that is possible to be done under the circumstances.

Second, Pathological actions which require to be modified or altered by medication.

THIRD LAW. Toleration by instinct. Perhaps this term might be improved. It is used to represent a vital law or sub-principle which is manifested on the part of the nerves of sensation, and is the very opposite of activity; that is, the usual material which primarily occasions the nerve of sensation to communicate a knowledge of its presence to the ganglionic centres, where an instinctive impulse to activity is generated, seems to be suspended. Thus the very causes which primarily induce pathological or diseased action are tolerated without the usual special disturbance.

This principle, peculiar to organic instinct, is no fancy picture to supply a connecting link in theory, but is illustrated in the person of the tobacco user, opium eaters, and drinkers of alcoholic stimulants, — the quantities which primarily caused great disturbance cease to occasion the usual effect. This is not due to any peculiarity in the article used, but dependent wholly on the toleration which the nervous system adapts itself to, and is frequently expressed by the illiterate as the result of second nature.

This law is for the purpose of self-preservation, and fulfills a very important relation to the welfare of the individual.

What does it express? We must admit that tobacco, opium, and alcohol are not material used by the organic powers for nutritive or physiological purposes; consequently it is the duty of the instinctive presiding power to generate that impulse to activity which more specially eliminates this material. The performance of this special duty involves a sacrifice of more or less of the accumulated organic force or power; and if the same cause, so long as applied, should occasion the generation of this special activity, the organic system would exhaust itself and die much quicker than it would to tolerate its presence and cease to make a special effort for elimination, thereby allowing the material to be eliminated by undisturbed action, in the usual manner of effete matter, as the best that can be done under the circumstances.

This is a wise law of instinct, and is a self preservative one.

Again, this principle is noticeable in persons residing in malarious districts, and in the filthy streets of our cities; the causes which are every day experienced by the residents, without developing active disease, will not be tolerated by a healthy nervous system fresh from the rural districts. The inhabitants tell him he must get "acclimated," or in other words his nervous system must become tolerant.

As important as this law is, for the welfare of the individual, it often proves annoying as well as mysterious to the physician who long continues the use of one kind of medicine. I recently chanced to be present at a New England Medical College of much distinction, during a lecture on *Materia Medica;* the subject was "Ergot and its powers." It was said that "the same preparation of ergot often acted finely for a period, but would perhaps lose its power, or certainly seem to, although the bottle had remained corked and properly cared for — and how that power escaped, or why it ceased to act, the Professor confessed was a problem which would have to wait until medical science could explore deeper those mysteries which surround us."

This law of toleration is a wise provision ordained to palliate the sins of our ignorance. It is the best which can be done under the circumstances for the individual welfare; it obviates to a limited extent those results, which ungovernable circumstances would otherwise occasion. It retards and postpones the effects of certain causes, which the will should exclude, but does not, and the instinct would desire to remove, but cannot. It is the safety sentinel on guard between instinct and intellect.

Again, this same principle of toleration modifies many diseases, and with some is the law which measures the time of self-limited disease; very distinctly recognizable in pneumonia, when induced by extremes of temperature, as will be mentioned hereafter.

In certain inflammatory troubles, it is the law which marks the period for the commencement of recovery, and is the essential condition to induce early by medication, for the safety of the patient.

Opium aids in the modification of excessive vital action, and lessens the severity and time of continuation, by facilitating a condition similar to toleration; we might say with propriety that certain doses produce artificial toleration; that is, the presence of the opium in the blood comes in contact with the nerves of sensation, and its presence unfits the nerve from performing its function of sensation. Sensation augmented is irritability and pain; which is relieved, and the sensation thus diminished is a temporary toleration, which permits the same causes to exist in contact with nerve fibre; yet the generated impulse to activity is not developed; thus the action is mitigated.

Also, the principle of toleration is the key to relapsing fever; a certain amount of struggle in the organic system is followed by a subsidence of the paroxysms, and the case has a fair outlook for recovery. After a period of rest a relapse ensues.

The explanation is this: the material causes of the fever were so plenty, or the system so enfeebled, that the law of toleration was established, which afforded a rest; after which the vital struggle recommenced, with a view to expel the cause.

This principle is a factor in a large variety of problems which come under the notice of a physician; and without a knowledge of it and its relations to *materia medica* and the cause of disease, it becomes impossible to effect a true solution of the phenomena we witness.

The already mentioned special laws of vital force, which become responsible for certain events, are *not all* we have to offer as belonging to this department, but comprise the more general principles; and under the heads of special disease it will be necessary to draw on those mentioned, as well as principles belonging more particularly to the case considered.

The reader may at this point infer that I am desirous of recovering the *vis medicatrix naturæ* theory of the vitalists, originated by Von Helmont, and previously included in Hippocrates' teachings. If the reader will inform himself of the condition of thought, by those early writers, in relation to the recognition of a vital principle, he will learn that they accomplished nothing, carried out no plan, recovered nothing but a vague idea that there was a vital principle, and that it played some part in the human system. They did not comprehend that they were entertaining and perpetuating an error by claiming an inherent power in medicine, but they also entertained the idea that there was a vital principle, which possibly might in some manner aid in the treatment of disease, and they thought it proper to define this principle as being possessed of a power like medicine — which they supposed had a power — and they applied to it the term *vis medicatrix naturæ* (medical power in nature).

Thus medical philosophers theoretically endowed medicine with a power, and subsequently finding that the vital power executed activities precisely similar to what they supposed the medical power fulfilled, they named the vital power, when thus manifested, *vis medicatrix naturæ*, which is a very improper term in our science. It is very plain that the term was coined to express a principle or power of the human organism, which could execute duties not physiological; the idea was correct, but the principle was erroneously named, and has thus been handed down to us, which is about all that has been done or learned in relation to it.

To illustrate how medical authors dispose of this principle, we quote from "Human Physiology," by John William Draper, M. D., LL. D., Professor of Chemistry and Physiology in the University of New York, page 111. "That fancied power, the vis medicatrix naturæ, is only an ideal expression of the perfection with which the various eliminating mechanisms work. Poisonous agents, whether they have been introduced from without, or have originated from morbid actions within, like all useless or noxious products, find their proper channel of escape, and the system will thus rid itself of intoxicating liquids and narcotic drugs if their quantity does not exceed the amount that it can destroy or excrete in a special period of time."

The stand-point of view, from which the foregoing

statement was made, was on the basis of vital power, which executes various duties for the human organism, and is correct.

Says Robley Dunglison, M. D., author of "General Therapeutics and Materia Medica," Professor of Institutes of Medicine in Jefferson Medical College of Philadelphia, formerly Professor of Materia Medica in the Universities of Virginia and Maryland, vol. i., page 37: "The existence, then, of such an instinctive power can neither be denied nor lost sight of in the treatment of disease. The error has been, that undue weight has been attached to it, so that the practitioner was altogether guided by its manifestations. . . . . The followers of Stahl — the great apostle of the doctrine — supposed a power to be present in the system of repelling morbific influences, and of reëstablishing equilibrium when disturbed. There are but few cases, however, in which trust can be safely placed in this power. It too often happens that diseased action in a tissue goes on augmenting until the functions of other tissues become deranged by extension of morbid action, or by sympathy, and disorganization and death follow. We often hear, for example, of 'efforts of nature,' yet the ideas attached to the expression are very unprecise. . . . . Yet, although we may discard the notion of efforts of nature, there is no doubt that good occasionally results from spontaneous discharges." — *Vide* page 39.

"Theory is the mental process which binds observed facts or phenomena together, compares them with each other, and deduces appropriate rules of practice. It is to theory that we are indebted not only for full, practical usefulness, but for every science. Facts are, doubtless, the elements of science, but the science itself does not exist, until these facts have been brought together, sifted and compared, and great general principles or laws deduced therefrom." What does Dr. Dunglison do with this "instinctive power," which should not be "lost sight of," which has had an "undue weight attached to it," "which we cannot trust," and "may discard the notion," yet "good occasionally results from it," and is a "fact" which should be "sifted," "and great general principles or laws" should be "deduced therefrom?" Professor Dunglison has shed no additional light on the principle; but the contrary, he has dragged it into more difficult surroundings, and bid us beware of its untrustworthiness.

This confusion is the result of looking at it from a wrong stand-point. He is an author of a *Materia Medica* instead of Physiology, and is instructing his readers in relation to medical power instead of vital power.

Stahl and others thought that if this power was ordained to execute important duties for the organism, that it necessarily must be endowed with a principle of guidance that would occasion it to *always* manifest itself harmoniously with the best interests of the individual. Experience taught their followers that this power could not always be trusted; therefore, this fact occasioned medical philosophers to set this principle completely aside in their theories, and instead of associating the will power, or sensibility with this principle, to guide it, they associated their will or sensibility with a supposed power in medicine, to guide and control the actions of organic life. Medical philosophers overlooked the fact that the instinctive and intellectual powers were all the powers that could be applied to the organic machinery; not recognizing the instinct and the laws, which modify its manifestations, they endowed medicine with a power, manifested by a code of laws peculiar to itself, which was theoretically made to take the place of that involuntary power which the Creator had endowed to man. Medicine as a material is the *cause,* which occasions the instinctive power to thus manifest itself; but medicine has no inherent power which executes those actions by virtue of its own ability.

It seems plain that the organic duty would be vested by the Creator primarily in the instinctive power; instead of in medicine, secondarily; which should execute duties independent of the will, in fulfillment of physiological and pathological actions.

If this instinct was both instinct and intelligence, there would be no occasion ordained in nature which would require a medical profession. The fact that the instinctive power is not intelligent, but is guided and directed by the intellect, indirectly, by using those articles of materia medica which will occasion this power to manifest itself for the better interests of the individual, constitutes the necessity of a medical profession.

Dr. Dunglison says " the great error consists in depending on this power." The error is not in this direction, but consists in expecting intellectual abilities or nothing from this power, when it possesses only instinct; thus as a power, if it fails to execute its actions intelligently, to the best interests of the individual, we are instructed to set it aside and use the artificial invention, medical power. We have not used any such power, even when we think we have, for there is none, although we have been made to believe that we did. We have administered those medicines which it was proper to administer, which have occasioned this instinctive power to act as was best to act, thus practicing right, but theorizing wrong, and were deceived into the belief that the medicine occasioned this change by virtue of its own power. In conclusion, vitality being a fixed force in nature which establishes human identity, must necessarily be governed by some laws peculiar to itself; we cannot make laws for its guidance, but possibly may comprehend the law of its obedience; and the knowledge of this law correctly set forth constitutes a correct theory of the only power capable of giving motion to living tissues.

A knowledge of the laws of vitality, or the laws of nature manifested through the human individual, constitutes the most essential acquisition required by the medical profession. It is a subject omitted in medical literature, not found in our text books, and assigned a position beyond our reach. There is, however, a silent conviction of thought, in the minds of some profound thinkers, that this secret principle or law of vital force, so long unrecognized, will at some future day illuminate the pathway of science, although that much desired revelation is placed far in the distance, and is thus expressed: "That this generation and generations to come will have passed to their everlasting rest before a discovery of the secret of vital activity is made." Says Henry Maudsley, M. D., F. R. C. P.: "It is easy to perceive how impossible it is in the present state of science, to come to any positive conclusion with regard to the nature of the vital force."

I believe that medical men can understand the nature of vital force in this generation, as well as they now do the nature of the force of gravitation. The reason medical men do not understand the nature of vital force is not because the subject is so profound, or the profession so superficial, it is because they have not looked in the right direction, — they have been studying the phantom " power in medicine," instead of the law of vital force.

CHAPTER IV.

THE APPLICATION OF THE THEORY OF VITALITY.

DISEASE.

THE term *Disease* is an expression of relations which vital force manifests under certain circumstances. It is used in a general and also a specific sense. A precise definition is not within the limits of possibility, because the term is not expressive of an entity, but of relations involving quite dissimilar principles. The principle involved in acute disease may be very unlike that which is present in chronic, as will be noticed under cachectic disease.

Life is the manifestation or action of vital force, and may be normal or abnormal. Normal action perpetuates the conditions of structure, through which life may be manifested until the natural period of organic dissolution. Abnormal action may change the structure of any tissue or organ, and thus render it unfit to perform normal actions, abridging its capabilities, causing decrepitude and death.

What is the nature of disease? or, in other words, what is the principle involved in the manifestation of disease? The reply to this question, as it will be here given, is more specifically applicable to acute disease, and may or may not be applicable to certain chronic disease.

We are to consider the human system as an organic body, endowed with special life force or power; also how we are related to the external or material world; that is, what are the ultimate, unlike, special vital properties, which in the aggregate constitute the sum total we call vitality, and what is the ordained executive duty which this *force* is commanded to fulfill.

We cannot define or recognize, through the manifestations of life, anything anterior to sensation, sensibility, and motion. We can define certain qualities of our nature consequent to these properties, although they cannot be expressed except through these three properties; therefore, those properties are what enable all the manifestations, of the relations of force to matter.

This vital force was ordained in the beginning to fulfill the instinctive or selective duty of putting together or forming organic bodies out of, perhaps, we might say, formless material. That is, the selective ability or instinctive wisdom appropriates unto its own individual use certain material to perpetuate each distinct individuality, and eliminates the same from the system after it has fulfilled the designed purpose, thus manifesting a principle of self-preservation independent of the will.

Also, this same force is endowed with a limited self-preservative ability to repair mechanical injuries and eliminate foreign material; the foreign material may be eliminated by the undisturbed depurative functions, or a special effort may be made with a view to its elimination.

THE APPLICATION OF THE THEORY OF VITALITY. 51

This special effort to eliminate may act for the best interest of the individual, which the circumstances will permit; or this action may be very unwise and detrimental to individual welfare, and require the superintendence of sensibility. This action, however, constitutes the disease.

This ability is an ordained duty for self-preservation of the individual, and nothing more. The organic force or vitality was ordained to fulfill the preservation of the individual, both by appropriating useful material and rejecting the non-usable, thus establishing, maintaining, and perpetuating an existence for the development of the highest order of His creation.[1]

Every motion or action in living tissue is a manifestation of the special property *contractibility*. This contractibility receives the impulse to move, either by a generated instinct or will.

The instinct exercises its duty through a knowledge, (if we may use the term) acquired by contact through sensation. Whatever material comes in contact with the nerves of sensation, becomes known to the presiding power, *instinct*, which issues the organic mandate to put into activity physiological actions if the material is a nutrient, all things being equal, that is, the supply with the wants. If the material thus brought in contact with the nerves of sensation is not a nutrient, and non-usable, or, in brief, foreign material, and if the said material

---

[1] The special action of vital force in relation to non-nutrient material or poison, which constitutes disease, has been attributed in theory to an action dependent on an *inherent power* in *this said* dead or inorganic material.

is classed as inert (to be hereafter mentioned) and small in quantity, it may be eliminated by the undisturbed depurative functions.

But if the material has a more antagonistic relation to the individual welfare, the instinct generates an impulse which puts into motion actions called pathological, or disease.

I trust the foregoing brief explanation of the premises and principles involved in the manifestations of that vital action we call disease, will enable the reader to more readily understand what may be the cause of disease.

CAUSES OF DISEASE.

A large quantity of food may be the cause, which if not possible to be digested, some other action must dispose of.

Retained excrementitious matter, decomposed animal or vegetable matter, certain chemical compounds formed at the breaking up of previous organized bodies,— the varieties are almost innumerable, — chemical compounds from the laboratory, simple elements, morbid vital products produced in the system, all may become a cause.

Chemical action within the system may multiply and produce a cause; also, certain degrees of temperature, not sufficient to cause destruction of tissue, may be a cause of disease, even of pneumonia.

The will or mind, when we take into consideration that instinct generates an impulse which sets into activity actions both normal and abnormal, and the close relation which the will force manifests to the organic force, — it is easy to comprehend that its influence may disturb the harmony of instinctive action, and occasion the angered mother's milk to be so elaborated that the compound becomes a poison to the child, that is, the milk is so perverted in its organization that the vital powers of the child cannot digest and assimilate it.

Through this source of mental modification of the various organic forces, very much good or evil may accrue to the patient, and the importance of this adjuvant to success deserves much attention.

In brief, whatever material that is developed or brought within the limits of organic life, so as to be recognized by the instinctive organic sense termed *sensation*, if not usable for physiological purposes, may, either from quantity or kind, become a *cause* for a disturbed vital action, denominated disease. This constitutes, briefly, the nature, principle, and cause of disease in general.

The order of this disturbed or pathological action forms the basis for name and nosology, or the classification of disease.

To illustrate the contrast between a theoretical basis which explains disease on a *one* power theory, or the *two* power theory, I quote the following from a writer of some distinction: "Scientific men, laboring in the field of medical chemistry, should strive to study the properties and habits of this proximate principle of disease, basing their application upon the simple and harmonious law of the correlation of forces."

This is a fair sample of those expressions made by the *two power* philosopher in urging some one to solve the riddle, *disease*. This expression seems to be a plunge in the dark to grasp a principle the whereabouts of which is unknown as to what family of philosophy it is kin. "Correlation of forces," which implies two forces, is what medical men have been studying for centuries, but have never met with any success.

A laborer in the field of chemistry is not so well qualified to solve this problem as one laboring in the field of physiology. Disease has no "habits or properties," but vital force has both, and disease is one of the sequences of its manifestations under certain circumstances.

In any other department mankind would become discouraged, and cease to apply those same principles to explain a phenomena which has so universally been attended with failure, and would try a different code. Custom alone keeps them in this channel.

THEORY OF INFLAMMATION.

Among the simple causes of inflammation may be mentioned a mechanical injury; effete or foreign matter retarded in the process of circulation in the more dense tissues of the joints; extreme degrees of temperature, either hot or cold; in brief, some condition or contact with the nerves of sensation, which occasions a very *unlike* sensation from the normal one. Inflammatory action must always be preceded by an *abnormal sensation*. All abnormal sensations are not followed by inflammatory action, but inflammatory action is never established without such a precedence.

Abnormal sensations must necessarily precede a large variety of morbid or pathological actions; therefore, a *cause* implies only a condition, which may occasion an *abnormal sensation* by virtue of contact alone; there is no *power* in the cause. The *sensation* which precedes pathological action may be known to the instinct alone, and oftentimes to both the instinct and the intellect.

The factors of this problem consist, first, of a *sensation;* second, what the instinct does in relation to such a sensation, which is to send an increased volume of blood to the part; thus the surroundings augment heat, fullness, and pain, or increased abnormal sensation.

Why does the instinct thus behave? Why not let the cause alone? In some particular instances, perhaps, the let alone policy might be preferable, but the ordained plan of life consists in the exercise of a selective ability of instinct to appropriate and reject material according to its usefulness or otherwise; and this instinctive wisdom has the one special faculty of knowing only by sensation.

Thus, the action maintained depends on the sensation. Were this sensation and instinct negligent to duty, our system would soon fill up and die from an overfullness or mechanical impediment.

Third. If the increased supply of blood, heat, fullness and pain surrounding the part are abnormal, why does not this very condition *also cause* an abnormal sensation and a new cause for a repetition of the same vital action, thus reproducing itself. *Such is the fact.*

Granting these premises, when will this kind of action cease, and what principle in vital law will explain it? It is explained by the law of toleration, which permits certain causes, which primarily occasioned vital disturbance, to maintain a continued contact without a special vital resistance. Thus, the law of toleration measures the duration of *some* self-limited diseases.

The extreme of this toleration is partially illustrated in the case of some ulcers, where increased action of the part, by irritation or heat, becomes necessary to develop the healing process.

PNEUMONIA.

This disease affords an opportunity to illustrate that a sensation, induced by temperature, may become a cause; also, that the disease will continue to run its period of self-limit, even when the primary cause has been removed early.

From Aitken's Practice on the Subject of Pneumonia, I quote: " Of 409 cases, 101 are referred distinctly to a chill as a cause. [Chromel, Barth, Grisolle.]" This cause does nothing except present a temperature which is abnormal, or, in other words, the temperature occasions an abnormal *sensation* to the nerves, which manifest that vital property.

Now, when we have established an abnormal sensation to a certain extent, then follows that action, manifesting the disease we call pneumonia. We must have the sensation first, although it may be known to the instinct alone.

With pneumonia, as with simple inflammation, the theoretical factors of the problem are the same. First, a sensation which may be caused in various ways; for instance, poison, produced by previous disease; steel dust or chill, each of which affords an unlike sensation to that class of nerves. Where the *cause* is a chill, the *cause* is soon removed, but the pneumonia becomes developed. How? The sensation occasions an instinctive impulse of blood to the parts, producing heat, congestion, and pain, which *secondary causes* supply a sensation that keeps up the inflammatory action, until the law of *toleration* permits a subsidence of activity.

With this view of the premises, what would be the inference in regard to treatment?

First, we are to consider that the danger in this disease is increased both by the amount of structure involved, and the great degree of heat developed. The latter is in proportion to the severity of the action, but not necessary to the amount of structure involved. Death may ensue from a large amount of territorial inflammation, or from a small amount, if the degree of temperature is sufficient to occasion the death of the part.

A chill being the first cause, is easily removed from our consideration; but it has occasioned a series of secondary causes, *congestion*, *heat*, and pain, which we must medicate, with a view to *diminish* the degree of each *cause;* thus conducting this self-limited disease through its course with less *heat* and less *pain* and congestion; to occasion the loss of heat by evaporation, and drinking of ice-water if desired, and opiates to diminish the sensation, constitute the more primary rational appliances.

FEVER.

A fever may be caused by retained excrementitious matter, that is an ephemeral fever, so called. The common continued fever may be caused by a variety of materials from various sources, which have gained access to the human organism; continued fevers, from a specific cause like scarlatina, measles, small-pox, and typhoid, are dependent on a *specific kind* of cause, in relation to which the vital powers behave in each individual in a quite similar manner.

Divesting the particular *cause* of all *power*, we are not to inquire how *a particular poison acts*, and what are the *laws* of its action, but simply what is the general and special manner of behavior of instinctive vital force under certain circumstances. With a view to establish the correctness of my theory of only one power involved in pathological action or disease, and that a vital one, it is unnecessary to mention all the special morbid structural changes attending vital disturbance in any particular disease, but merely the general characteristics involved in the particular disease. There is no one particular distinguishing system which always enables the observer to determine that the given case is a fever, or a particular kind of a fever; but a variety of morbid processes becomes necessary for the applying of the term legitimately, also some special symptoms to distinguish the kind. The more distinguishing kind of vital disturbance, which designates continued fever, consists of a disturbance of the whole system, in the order of a cold, hot, and sweating period, each manifested more or less distinctly with different degrees of prominence, each period being manifested twice in the twenty-four hours.

In intermittent fever (fever and ague), those three periods are manifested only once each day, and then it is called *quotidian;* when the paroxysm occurs every second day, it is called *tertian;* every third day, that is, skipping two days between the attacks, a *quartan*. Remittent fever is distinguished from intermittent by an indefinite *time* which is taken to produce the paroxysms of the three stages, which may be executed anywhere from twelve to thirty hours; also, the remission or period of rest between paroxysms may be from six to thirty-six hours, according to the strength of the patient. Relapsing fevers consist in a manifestation of two paroxysms a day, of the cold, hot, and sweating stages, for a period of seven to seventeen days (these odd numbers are very much like a whim), and then the paroxysms cease for an indefinite period of several days to two weeks, and then follows a recurrence of the paroxysms, as at first.

These periods of special activity and rest may be continued four or five times. Measles, scarlatina, and small-pox have, additional to the continued paroxysm, a distinguishing eruption, and the propagation seems due to a special or specific cause; likewise, typhoid fever.

What do medical authors do with this variety of febrile action? They give us an accurate and valuable account of all the symptoms and structural morbid changes, and the kind of cause; followed by a brief recital of the different kinds of power inherent in the various kinds of poisons or *cause ;* and plunge more or less into the theory of the activity of this foreign power, according to their enthusiasm, caution, and previous success. In pursuing the theory, they soon find themselves swimming in thin air, without good anchorage, and paddle back with an entire change of countenance, and feelingly express that these things are not all settled yet; that medical science is still in embryo; but admonish us to be good observers, watchful and attendant, and treat the case on general acknowledged principles.

It is asserted that we cannot comprehend the laws, and much less the principle or workings, of the forces in nature which relate to our material organism; but we *must treat* the *case* on *general principles*. These general principles constitute the very ideas which we are in pursuit of; and in searching for them I differ from others in claiming that they are found in, and belong to, the vital force alone, instead of any foreign force or power.

In the commencement of a fever, we generally notice first an ushering in chill. The chill may be experienced by the patient, and at the same time an increased temperature is indicated by the thermometer; sooner or later an increased determination of blood and an augmented temperature is apparent in the skin.

The language of this instinctive action is an effort to effect elimination through the skin. This action is controlled by instinct, and may overdo its labor; that is, the fullness of the capillaries may close the pores and retard the elimination, until a gradual subsidence of this activity, when the sweating stage is established; and as this activity of force subsides, the so-called cold stage is experienced.

These alternations of *activity* and *repose* of this power are repeated twice in twenty-four hours, in continued fever, with more or less distinctness and variation of time assigned to each stage. The principle involved, is to deterge from the organic system something which does not belong there; and when this order of disturbance exists, we call the existing disease some kind of fever.

All of the other attending symptoms are in evidence of perverted vital power, important to notice and alleviate, but not in any manner detracting from the general plan of the organic powers to eliminate material not usable for physiological purposes.

INTERMITTENT FEVER. — FEVER AND AGUE.

This fever is, unquestionably, caused by malaria or a material which has an origin more particularly in new settled lands, and of presumed vegetable origin. After residing in such a district a certain period many persons become acclimated, which means only the establishment of the principle or law of toleration, whereby the cause ceases to occasion this special disturbance. The principle or theory of vital action is the same, in case only one paroxysm of a cold, hot, and sweating period occurs in twenty-four hours, or in case it occurs only every second or third day.

Why this variation? All power has a limit to its capabilities, and the continued existence in the presence of the cause necessarily implies a continued tax on the depurating power; and when the accumulation of the material within the system becomes sufficiently increased, a special effort or febrile paroxysm is developed, usually of much violence. The degree of activity and the enfeebled powers in this particular manner require more or less repose, and the recuperative ability of this power to establish another paroxysm, measures the time or day when it shall be manifested.

The enlarged liver and spleen, called ague cakes, so common in miasmatic localities, are in consequence of a disturbed vital action, occasioned by the circulation of the foreign material through those organs.

REMITTENT FEVER,

As before mentioned, is also another variety of vital disturbance occurring in the same locality as intermittent fever, and from the same cause, paludal poison, involving the same theory, but manifested in paroxysms of differently measured time.

RELAPSING FEVER.

This fever does not differ essentially from the usual manifestations of continued fever; its peculiarity consists in running a certain length of time, when all the paroxysms cease for several days, a week, or more, and then commence again and continue for a period, possibly recurring from three to five times. Additional to the fever theory there is nothing of importance as theory, except the law of either toleration or prostration, manifested in this particular disturbance, which affords the vital powers a period of rest.

ERUPTIVE FEVERS.

Eruptive fevers are not different in theory, although their cause is different and of a specific character; and the manner of propagation and general appearances furnish additional material for study.

TYPHOID FEVER.

There is nothing in connection with this fever in opposition to the primary principles involved in febrile diseases; although the many attending symptoms and consequences make this disease a source of much anxiety to both physician and friends. The cause is generally conceded to be of animal origin, although what that material is in the abstract, is not yet determined; there is very much, however, in connection with typhoid fever, of importance to learn, which is now involved in mystery. It seems that the cause of this disease requires a certain period of incubation, prior to its more general effect. " The living human body, therefore, is the soil in which the specific poison breeds and multiplies."

It seems conclusive that whatever the first poison may be, its own bulk does not constitute the sum total of the material with which the vital powers have to contend; but it affords a primal cause for a series of changes which multiply the amount of specific poison within the system.

Repudiating the idea that we are to study *how this poison acts*, we have legitimately before us to consider only its origin; how it multiplies itself; is it diffused, and how; and how is it communicated; and the behavior of vital force in relation to the cause.

This department of inquiry is not my special subject, although I do not wish to pass it over without expressing my immature views, which may call out better and more exact information. What may be known of the origin of the cause is certainly, at present, mostly conjectural. The advocates of the germ theory claim that this poison is *always* generated in the intestines, from a previous germ which finds there the proper surroundings for reproducing itself.

This theory is fatal to itself in this particular application; because it leaves us without any knowledge how the *first* germ could have an existence. In this application, germ signifies a primary body, endowed with a principle capable of self multiplication or reproduction.

In distinction from other causes which may occasion disease, we can say with certainty that a germ is not a product of chemical force nor a morbid vital product of organic action. But should we determine how the poison is multiplied it may throw some light on its origin.

We have evidence to convince us that the *cause* or poison is multiplied within the human system; and setting aside the *germ cause* for the present, we have remaining only two sources through which a multiplication of poison can be effected within the human system.

First, vitiated vital products, from perverted vital action. Second, chemical changes.

First, it is known that the anger of a nursing mother may alter the formation of the milk and change it to a poison; and it is rational to believe that a large variety of elaborated fluids acquire an existence through perverted vital action, which, in turn, are a *cause* of further vital perversions; and in this way a human organism may commit suicide.

It seems consistent to believe that vitiated vital products afford, at least, a class of *secondary causes* in many diseases which largely occasion the augmentation of irregular vital force.

It is extremely difficult to see how such products could be a *primary* cause of typhoid, or even be the communicating contagion through which the disease is propagated;

for like germs, where do we get the first vitiated product?

Without any known means of obtaining the *first* vitiated vital product, I am persuaded to reject, also, the vital multiplying agency; and shall examine the only remaining, namely, the chemical, which agency unquestionably, often is the productive power which furnishes material cause for vital disturbance. Previous to the examination of the multiplying ability of chemical agency in this particular disease, it becomes of importance to inquire whether typhoid fever is a local disease with a general secondary disturbance, or a general disease with a special local lesion.

The germ theorists claim that the primary cause is always local and confined to the intestines, therefore the disease is local; and very many of the medical profession claim that typhoid fever is a local disease, without entering into controversy whether the cause remains local or otherwise.

It seems that if we can prove the primary cause to inhabit the intestines only, we have better ground for calling the disease a local one; but if we become satisfied that the primary, specific cause becomes diffused over the whole system, we must accept the disease as one of general character with special local lesions.

Those who have perseveringly sought to learn the manner in which typhoid poison is communicated assure us that the swallowing of the virus is the only means by which it can be received into the system. Acknowledging that even one case has been communicated by the swallowing of water containing the poison, which premises are, doubtless, acceptable to all, furnishes us a starting-point for a tangible theory. Take into consideration that this poison in water must either be soluble or insoluble; if insoluble, a microscopic vision only can reveal it. If insoluble, and so very diminutive as to require the aid of a microscope to discern it, and perhaps not discernible at that, it must, certainly, have a very remarkable *fixed* character, as the chemists call it, not to be susceptible of solution; for cohesion and solution are opposing forces in chemistry, and whatever weakens cohesion favors solution; thus the pulverizing of a substance tends much toward its solution.

If the poison is insoluble, it cannot be absorbed, for through the power of solubility *only* is any substance rendered capable of absorption.

Water is the natural solvent which holds in solution all material which goes to supply the wants of the organism, as well as all those substances which are circulated in contact with nerve tissue, thus becoming the cause of vital disturbance.

Not only would it be remarkable to have such a fixed body, but if the poison is insoluble, and was introduced into the system by swallowing, we have the best of reasons for adopting the theory that the cause remains locally in the intestines.

Again, if the poison is insoluble, we have to consider that it occasions a vital disturbance, either by mechanical impediment or as a local irritant. It is certainly not the former; therefore, if the latter, with its local habitation, it must necessarily be attended with very severe primary local disturbance, before the secondary general febrile

THE APPLICATION OF THE THEORY OF VITALITY. 67

paroxysms are developed. The facts, however, in the order of the symptoms, are the very opposites.

Again, if the cause is insoluble, and not absorbable and microscopic in its character, and to be largely multiplied in the system, we have before us a material which is distressingly incomprehensible to imagine by what law peculiar to matter it may be multiplied, and what law peculiar to vital properties would make it a rational cause for so grave a disease as typhoid fever. The rational inference would be that such an insoluble, diminutive particle would pass along with the contents of the intestines and occasion no trouble.

The testimony elicited in support of the primary cause remaining in the intestines is far from satisfactory, and good sense dictates that we should abandon the belief of its local habitation or insolubility.

The kind of reasoning usually employed in support of the theory that typhoid fever is a local disease, as well as the kind of evidence which many physicians accept, "that we cannot with positiveness assert that any particular case is one of typhoid fever unless a post mortem reveals the evidence of local lesion," seems to be based on very narrow premises, namely, that if the cause is specific, which we all admit, and a local specific effect on Peyer's glands and other adjacent tissues is very liable, consequently, by virtue of the law of specifics (if there is any such law in vital behavior), unless the specific effect is present the specific cause could not exist, therefore the disease was not typhoid fever. A broad view of the premises involved, including the laws of vital force, and the laws peculiar to matter or the supplying cause of disease, evidently makes it incumbent on us to adopt a different plan of reasoning for the solution of this important problem.

In support of the doctrine that typhoid is a general disease, which may be, and often is, complicated with local lesion in the region of Peyer's glands, we have adopted the premises that the disease may be communicated by drinking water containing the special poison, and it requires no great violation of rational imagination to believe that this poison is held in solution; certainly, when we take into consideration that water is the great natural solvent, and that the cause, very probably, is of vegetable or animal origin; and what I mean by vegetable or animal origin is, that the material cause has been previously subjected to the forces peculiar to those two kinds of life before it takes on a retrograde condition or breaking up which renders it a poison.

The kinds of matter which are seized by these two forces are very far from being liable, while breaking up and forming new compounds, to enter into any *fixed* condition which is insoluble in water; consequently, we have the best of reasons for believing that the poison is held in solution.

Granting that the poison is soluble, it certainly must be absorbable; and if it is absorbable, the cause is very generally distributed over the system, and if thus distributed, we have the best of reasons for calling the disease a general one which may have local complications. In further support we have the continued febrile paroxysms like fevers, the *general* character of which we never question. Also the slow, insidious approach, with temperature slowly increased, is in evidence that the cause is small; and, as it becomes multiplied, more severe symptoms are manifested in various parts of the organism. In consideration of the foregoing premises, I am persuaded to adopt the conclusion that typhoid fever is a general disease.

We will now return to the examination of the several processes by which the poison may be multiplied, and consider the remaining unexamined chemical agency. The fertile field for imagination in this department is certainly very broad; but with a knowledge of the kind of force which seizes organized material after its vitality has surrendered it, we have a plausible outlook for the belief that the organic protean compounds, after being broken up, pass through a great variety of chemical unions, and by stronger affinities are again broken and reunited, and thus continue to change in the order of dissolution until the material is returned to its elementary condition.

During these series of changes it becomes quite plausible to admit that some of those changes might be productive of a specific poison, which material, taken into the human system and brought in contact with certain living plastic compounds, might occasion the death of the particular material, which then enters into chemical changes; or, perhaps, this change may occur with the previous disintegrated tissues; thus the law of chemical affinity being supplied with the material for perfecting the formation and multiplication of this specific virus within the human system.

There seems to be no doubt relative to the presumption that the multiplication of the specific cause of typhoid fever does take place within the living, human organism, and microscopic examinations fail to furnish us with the evidence that it is by an increase of monads, spores, infusorial animalcules, fungus germs, or bacteria; and after a careful examination of all the premises in the case, together with the different known means by which any such multiplication could be effected with the material organism, we are persuaded, after ruling out various negations, to adopt the most rational remaining basis, that the multiplication of this specific virus is effected by CHEMICAL AGENCY.

It is very difficult to avoid this conclusion; also that the material is soluble and absorbable and diffused throughout the entire system, and that the disease is general in its character. Whether the poison is first absorbed by the veins or the lacteals, or both; or whether this change is effected with disintegrated tissue or living material is surrendered by its vitality and enters into new relations; or whether the constituents of the blood become changed, or the blood is only the vehicle for transporting the poison as an additional material to the blood proper, are questions of a secondary importance, and, perhaps, difficult to determine. It is very practical to ask, How is typhoid fever communicated?

The supporters of the germ theory and many of the advocates of the doctrine of local disease, have demonstrated, beyond a doubt, that the disease is most frequently communicated by the discharges from the bowels; also, they represent that the blood of the typhoid fever patient, injected into the blood of animals, does not cause typhoid fever, but may cause death; therefore, take into consideration, in this statement, that this class of reasoners are very reluctant to call any case one of typhoid fever unless the local lesion is present.

Whether the poison is in a condition to be communicated otherwise than through the dejections and by swallowing, is a question I shall not attempt to discuss, although it is very important and of great practical value.

The poison being soluble, the vapors may contain it, and, by respiration, it would be possible to unite with the fluids of the fauces and be swallowed. We are credibly informed that the physicians in the typhoid wards of some European hospitals are so firm in the belief that the poison cannot be communicated except by swallowing, that they never swallow while in those wards, and rinse the fauces thoroughly after their exit, and are expected to escape the disease.

It is not to be supposed that all of the *causes* of vital disturbance are essentially the specific virus, for there is always a class of secondary causes in every fever which occasion variously modified activities. The fact that there is no necessary connection between the intensity of the febrile action and the extent of intestinal mischief is in corroboration of the increase of poison, independent of vital action. That it may be absorbed and carried in contact with nerve tissue, thus modifying the generated nerve force which controls the circulation in the region of local lesions, even to that extent which unfits the nerve force for maintaining the nutrient supply for its structural support, whereby, sooner or later, partial or complete perforation is effected from *atrophy*. This is consistent with the belief that the poison is circulated in the blood, and not inconsistent with any other fact or law of vital activity. The local lesions are generally considered the evidence of the presence of a primary specific poison; therefore, we may ask whether the *specific cause* or the *secondary* cause occasions the interruption of that nerve force which so frequently terminates in complete atrophy or perforation. If we attribute it to the secondary causes, we are making such cause the specific instead of the primary; and, again, how do we account for the rose-colored spots on the abdomen, which are regarded as pathognomonic of typhoid, if the specific poison is not in the blood? These spots are also evidence of innervation from causes which can affect that region only by circulation, very rarely appearing before the end of the first week.

The gland of Peyer is not all of the structure involved in local lesions in that immediate vicinity, but is more liable to be thus affected because a gland is a more highly endowed structure, and will experience less perversion of disturbed action and maintain its structural organization than other kinds of tissue.

The manner in which vital force behaves in relation to this specific poison, implies the characteristic appearances manifest in this particular disease, which disturbance is always quite similar, and affords the evidence of the specific cause.

Observation alone does not constitute all of our available means for acquiring a better knowledge of typhoid fever; but much must be effected through processes of inductive reasoning; a knowledge of certain laws enables us to draw a better inference in regard to what we observe, and law may determine facts which would otherwise be difficult to discover. Thus, mathematical calculation, based on a known law, made it very probable that an undiscovered planet existed in a certain position in the heavens, and through the guidance of this law the telescope was pointed in that direction, and the human eye, for the first time, saw the disc of Neptune.

The foregoing premises seem to furnish plausible evidence that the agency which multiplies the specific poison within the human organism is a chemical one; therefore the same agency outside of the body, in drains and cess-pools, may unite the elements of organic compounds which are breaking up under certain circumstances, and originate the specific poison.

The facts that this poison is so frequently communicated from fæcal matter and that swallowing will communicate the disease, are of great value; yet we consider that it is not proved that such is always the manner by which the disease is communicated, although it may be possible. Should it be proved that the poison must find ingress by swallowing, it will be a fact of great practical value.

TEMPERATURE.

All causes in acute disease occasion an amount of vital disturbance, all things being equal, in accordance with the degree of morbid sensation which they produce, in contact with the nerves which express that special, vital property. Therefore an increased temperature of the blood becomes a *secondary cause* of no small importance, and, in all acute disease, an increased temperature occasions an increased disturbance of the vital energies. The degree of temperature alone, when augmented to a certain extent, perverts vital action in such a manner as to cause death. Some organisms will endure more heat than others, but early anticipated danger is in no manner so correctly foretold as by the temperature indicated by the thermometer.

Experience has taught many practitioners that in all febrile diseases, particularly scarlatina, measles, and typhoid fever, the *severity* and danger are much less when especial *early* attention has been given to keeping the temperature reduced by baths or the wet sheet pack, which is always available. One reason for the better success is due to diminishing the cause, and a very important duty is also aided by this treatment in effecting the depuration of effete matter and the increased accumulation from interstitial change, allowing it to escape more rapidly through those emunctaries, which are less liable to be further disturbed by its egress.

The many morbid vital products and phenomena, dangerously increased by this secondary cause, temperature, are too numerous to mention, and if there is one consideration in the treatment of acute disease, more important than any other, it is the diminishing of the temperature. Envelop the patient several times a day in a wet sheet pack, for twenty to forty minutes, in a temperature not cold but agreeable to the patient. The thermometer only should be a test of necessity or success, and attention *early* in scarlatina is of paramount importance. Many cases, that otherwise would be fatal, may be cured by the continued diminished temperature. This is strong language, but the premises on which it is predicated vouch most emphatically for its correctness.

CONSTITUTIONAL OR CACHECTIC DISEASE.

There is a large class of maladies pertaining to the class of cachectic disease which are only very remotely involved in the principles more particularly the subject of this volume. To pass them by unnoticed would be equivalent in the judgment of some as recognizing in such, nothing antagonistic to the principles advocated; consequently, a reference thereto is more to assign a position than otherwise, although they occupy no small attention of the physician and make up a large share of the chronic affections with which we have to deal.

They are of more than minor importance, and the particular thought to be associated with them, is so unlike what we have been considering, that a special position must be afforded them, that they may not be confounded in association, or treated on the principles of more acute diseases.

"This class of diseases is preëminently distinguished as being caused by or attended with universal depravity of the organization, or general derangement of all the bodily functions, constituting, in fact, constitutional taint or malconformation which may be transmitted through many generations, with either increasing or decreasing intensity, as the voluntary habits of each successive generation are more or less in conformity with physiological laws."

What this "constitutional taint" may be, is a theme

for much inquiry; and, doubtless, most of us are easily persuaded that our ability to grasp the idea, is much less than we would desire.

Two persons of different families, reared under the same apparent influences, live in the same house, eat at the same table, breathe the same atmosphere, are exposed to the same vicissitudes, and have no unlike surroundings which give evidence to our senses of a material cause; yet one becomes vigorous and hardy, while the other goes into a state of decline and death from constitutional taint.

Under the head of cachectic diseases, it seems that we should look for a cause outside of a material one. In acute diseases we have been considering the laws of perverted vital action, occasioned by causes introduced from without, and change of material engendered within; but with cachectic diseases we are to consider a perversion of vital force, which, when supplied with good material and favorably surrounded, yet *makes a bad use of it*, perhaps develops a cancer or tubercle. In cachectic diseases, the vital force seems to use good material improperly, the elaborating influences or executive harmony is unbalanced. In acute disease, we have to consider a perversion of vital power, *after* it has fulfilled the duty of organization; with cachexia we are to consider the perversion of vital power, *while performing* the act of organization.

With this distinction between the fundamental principle involved in the two classes of disease, it is very easy to comprehend that we have a different class of duties to attend to, both in our philosophy and in our therapeutics.

This perversion of vital force during the process of organization is not alone confined to the human species, and animal kingdom, but is noticeable in the vegetable, in many of the grass tribe, and particularly in wheat and rye. The vital force in harmony with the laws peculiar to its designs, develops the perfect kernel of rye; this same force, perverted, develops the kernel of ergot in the place of the grain.

We are informed by the United States Dispensatory, that a "microscopic fungus has an existence independent of the morbid grain, growing entirely separate from it on various parts of the plant, also upon the surface of the ergot; and if this sporidia or white dust be applied to seeds before germination, or sprinkled in the soil at the roots of the plants, after they have begun to grow, it will give rise to ergotized fruit."

How many generations we can trace a cause of perverted force, to a material which is itself the product of a previous perversion, is difficult to determine. Ergot occasions a perversion of vital force in the human organism, although we use it in a manner to make it available; yet, if too much of the cause [ergot] be used, this perversion results in dry gangrene. To return to cachectic disease. We are to consider that a material cause alone is not responsible for the development of this class of disease; such may hasten their appearance and termination, but we must look more remotely to an impress, if we may use the term, stamped on the tendency of the power.

This condition of inherited primal tendency, considered in a certain sense illustrative of the idea, may be represented as an individual without the capital stock of vitality sufficient to contend equally with others in the race of life. They are compelled to more strictly conform to the straight and obedient requirements of physiological law.

They cannot endure those exposures which many of us do with apparent impunity. They are the living representatives of the truth, that obedience to law means life. Their slight (as it often is) violation of law is not the whole cause of decline; it is only the proximate, while the remote is the constitutional tendency.

There is much, very much, to consider about this class of maladies, although it is not my purpose to enter into such details; but a brief mention, of the indications for treatment may not be out of place.

One fact about this class of disease is an inability to use proper material properly; or, in other words, the system does not seem to appropriate the same amount of material from the same bulk, which a better endowed organization would accomplish; they require special feeding as well as a special regard to other laws. This special feeding and obedience to law constitutes the primal and *very important* part of the treatment.

Medication is a secondary appliance, useful to a degree; but remember, it is secondary. This distinction, I fear, is not always observed with the profession; and the doctrinal error, of *medical power*, has afforded ample opportunity for the development of quackery, and the supply to the patient of this *power in bottles,* to be substituted for vital power, in which the patient is most significantly deficient.

One reason may be assigned why the system does not

use more of the material supplied, — from a lack of ability to elaborate those fluids which aid in the various processes of digestion; consequently, we are to supply, not only the *special food*, but the *special aid* embodied in certain preparations which assist digestion.

Stimulants and tonics only indirectly aid such processes, never by assisting directly; but sometimes occasioning what there may be of vital power to be more generously manifested in a certain direction.

This kind of assistance is very liable to be overdone. In administering a supply to this class of disease, there should be kept in view the difference between a compound which is a product of vital organization and one which is a product of chemical agency. Vital force cannot appropriate ultimate elements or chemical compounds and convert them into tissue. The doctrine of chemical food is supported by many who believe in it, and who urge its administration, but there are good reasons in abundance to prove it a delusion. Such preparations may prove beneficial as medicine, but not as a food.

The use of ferruginous preparations affords the most convincing evidence of chemical food: although of great utility, such are not food, as will be hereafter noticed.

CHAPTER V.

MATERIA MEDICA.

EVERY science necessitates the coining of special terms to express those principles to be represented in each department; and the science of medicine, as taught, with its required Materia Medica, has sought to express principles pertaining to medicine in harmony with its supposed properties.

Medical science is based on certain presumed fundamental principles, among which is an adopted one that medicine has an active principle; that it is endowed with an inherent principle or power which can execute, by virtue of its own inherent ability, a momentum to vitalize tissues. This belief has become a constituent of the sum total of intellectual acquirements which make up a medical education; it is the idea talked and taught, and on which very much of the practice is predicated.

This idea to-day is as much a part of the man himself as the belief in a Christian religion; it fills an otherwise void in that chain of thought which he presupposes makes him a useful member of society; and so firmly is this belief stamped into his being, that all philosophy, medical and metaphysical, is made to bow and bend to this presumed principle. It gets out of the way for nothing; but everything is made to give place to this.

If the theory of vital force, previously presented, is correct, as I claim it to be, the doctrine of an inherent power in medicine is a fallacy of no small magnitude. There is no compromise in science, and it becomes us to determine whether this supposed inherent power in medicine is a God-given ordained power, or invented by man alone to afford a basis for theoretical explanation of problems in nature, which ancient man could not otherwise surmount. The latter is the whole fact.

It is an inheritance which we should no longer nourish and perpetuate; consequently, it becomes evident that we have terms as well as ideas associated with medicine which tend to confuse our thought and pervert our reasoning.

There being no inherent power in medicine, it becomes important to differently express its usefulness, more in harmony with its true relations to our organisms. The term, "active principle," or "inherent active property or power," does not express its relation, for this relation is not one of power; and the term should be expunged from our vocabulary.

It is very easy to discover how such language was introduced, when we take into consideration that vital power has different ways of manifesting itself, which are appropriately termed different vital properties, and which are expressed by specific names. Consequently, if vital power had different properties, it seemed equally appropriate to have the *power medical* also have properties or different ways of manifesting its inherent active principle or power.

The relation of medicine to the human organism being

one of *cause*, not power, its presence occasions vital power to behave unlike what it otherwise would. Thus one article may occasion *emesis*, another *diuresis*, and another stimulation; and instead of using the term, "active principle or medical property," to convey the relation of cause and effect, it would be much more appropriate to say its medical or medicinal relations caused the special effect; that is, such an article *occasions emesis*, etc., instead of saying that the medical power *acted* to produce any special effect.

In rearranging the plan of medical science, we have only to analyze our thoughts to their ultimate condition, of primitive ideas; recognize the ultimate first principle correctly; refuse to be conducted in the channel of traditional thought; arrange our synthesis, or putting together, so that facts and philosophy will blend. We have little or nothing to throw away; the material is all useful, but the edifice requires to be partitioned off in a different manner.

There are three grand divisions of material upon and with which the vital forces act, as follows: —

The first class are nutrients, and are acted on for the purpose of being assimilated.

The second class consists of material which is termed by the profession inert; that is, it neither contributes nutriment, nor by its presence occasions any special vital disturbance in any direction except by bulk, but merely abides the course of time, and becomes eliminated by the undisturbed depurative functions.

The third class comprises that vast array of material called medicine and poison, which, by its presence, occasions special vital efforts or actions.

The different manner in which vital force behaves in relation to this class of material affords that knowledge by which we know what use or injury may result from its administration. The degree of incompatibility is modified by the quantity, and may be mildly alterative, or violently poisonous; thus we are enabled by Sensibility to administer such medicines as will occasion the instinctive power to manifest itself more in harmony with the best interest of the patient. Give this plan of reconstructed science mature deliberation, inquire through the various means within your reach, whether such principles are supported and verified by human organisms; the premises are easily approachable, and are briefly included in the idea, whether vital power acts differently in relation to different kinds of material, or whether the various kinds of inorganic material possess special inherent powers which execute the life functions in the highest endowed organism ever created. The key which unlocks the door to correct medical science is expressed in this sentence.

ANÆSTHESIA.

Those conditions induced by certain articles of the Materia Medica, which occasion a suspension of sensation and sensibility, are not involved in any principles unlike what we have considered.

A certain quantity of alcoholic stimulus occasions an increased activity of the heart, and augments superficial circulation. If the quantity is increased to a certain extent, the presence of the alcohol renders the organic system unable to manifest the full expression of sensation and sensibility. This condition begins with the more voluntary abilities, and tends towards the involuntary: if the stimulus is increased sufficiently, there is a complete suspension of involuntary activities and death follows. Narcotics maintain the same relation; that is, certain quantities in contact with the nerve tissues, incapacitate such tissues from the manifestation of their primary legitimate functions; and we take advantage of such facts, to favor certain desired results in the treatment of the sick. Ether and chloroform more quickly occasion such conditions, with less of the intermediate disturbances, in the approach or recovery.

STIMULANTS.

Under this head a mention of alcoholic stimulus only will be briefly considered, not with a view of doing full justice to all of its relations to the people, but, more particularly as an article of Materia Medica. Is alcoholic stimulus a food — that is, is alcohol transformed into vitalized tissues — was a question which not many years since puzzled the brain of the physiologist.

It has been settled positively in the negative, and a more complex question succeeded it, namely, Is alcohol eliminated from the system as alcohol? Certain experiments were made which gave credence to this idea; but later experiments have proved that but a small per cent. is eliminated as alcohol, while the remainder is changed in the system and eliminated as a different substance. We are to consider alcohol more particularly in this place as a vehicle which is supposed to convey a power into the human system. No one article has been so highly endowed by human belief or so generally used by the community, for this purpose, as alcoholic stimulus. Our texts books have not definitely settled the manner of how this power or force is utilized; whether it contributes additional power to muscle, or nerve tissues; whether it runs the machinery of life alone, or jointly with the vital force; whether it executes physiological duties when vitality is weary, and after convalescence unselfishly takes itself out of the way, and surrenders the executive chair to the proper appointed vitality.

One author informs us " that there are conditions in which alcohol acts simply as material for the production of force, and may be looked upon as a food which requires no digestion, and sets free in a useful form its latent energy."

It is not strange, with this doctrine before the people, that intemperance continues to blight the prospects of our nation. It is not strange that moral suasion, praying, and legislation fail to turn the tide of this growing evil.

Whether alcohol is a food or is possessed of a power, is not determined by experiment and observation; the same kind of experiment and observation would make arsenic and antimony a food and give them a power as well as alcohol. We have mentioned in a foregoing chapter, the general law and processes through which material must be organized and the condition in which it must remain, in order to be susceptible of assimilation.

Alcohol is a chemical compound, and occasions certain special manifestations of vital force, which have been mistaken for the "latent agencies" of the alcohol.

Pleasurable feelings or sensations, and happiness of mind, are the result of normal activities, of a balanced functional action. Thus when a small quantity of stimulus is introduced into the system, it occasions an augmented and but slightly unbalanced vital activity, which promotes, with many, a sensation which is agreeable; the departure from normal activity not being sufficient to cause any unpleasantness. This sensation is called the nervine action of the alcohol; it should be called the exhilarative effect, instead of the action. Increase the quantity and the change of action is more apparent, the circulating system is implicated, the nerve exhilaration is less proportionally manifested; the heart's action is more frequent; more fullness to the pulse; increased capillary circulation, and heat to the surface. This is the stimulant effect. No power is added to vital power, or substituted for it it; nor any " latent energy set free." It is merely an illustration of how vital power behaves in relation to the material alcohol.

The degree of excitability in different nervous systems is absolutely independent of the *amount* of nervous force in the individual.

Stimulation is not an increase of the sum total of vital power which the individual may possess, but is an increase of vital power in a *certain direction*; the manifestation is one of expenditure of the stock on hand; yet it is of paramount importance that it should be thus manifested in certain cases, and thus it becomes the means of saving life.

This statement may seem paradoxical: to claim that the manifestation is an expenditure, and yet is often the means of saving life. For the purpose of illustration, we will introduce a fever patient suffering from prostration;

the condition of the patient is one of internal congestion, with a superficial deficiency of blood and coldness; the functions of life cannot be continued long, if this state of unbalanced circulation is permitted to remain. We have previously ascertained that alcoholic stimulus *occasions* an increased activity of the heart, and augments the superficial circulation.

Thus the system will endure this expenditure of vital power, with a more nearly balanced circulation, far better than it can endure the internal congestion, and deficiency of capillary circulation. The unbalanced circulation tends directly to death, and the restoration of the balance gives the patient another chance in the struggle for life. This waste of vital power, in this particular direction, is a choice of evils. Stimulants will not occasion the rallying of the life powers when the attending collapse is due to exhaustion, it is only applicable beneficially in prostration.

In relation to the use of alcohol for medicinal purposes, a certain eminent professor of Materia Medica (who believes in the inherent power) says: "It is well to do so for temporary use, for which you will feel better; but, if continued, ends in worse; the system soon goes into a rapid decline. It is like taking the material of a house to stop the leak; it will do for temporary emergency, but soon the house becomes worse by patching than if let alone, and perhaps past all value — not possible to mend." This deduction is the result of observation, in opposition to the belief of an inherent power, but strictly in harmony with the theory that alcohol contains no power. Some medical philosophers reason about the same premises from two different standpoints, and I will quote from one of those philosophers, a little theory on the basis of vital force. Says Dr. Brown-Sequard, " Now that we have passed in review all those facts showing that *nervous force* can be transformed into the other forces of nature that we know, almost all of them, the question arises, Can all the forces of nature be transformed into nervous force? This is one of the greatest questions that we could undertake to consider. Unfortunately, the elements we have for solving it are as yet very few. We do not know positively yet — at any rate, I do not."

Thus it seems that even if medicine has a power, or force, inherent in itself, the question is unsolved in his mind whether such force can be transformed into nerve force. His opinion is of value. He is a thinker of high order.

No one article of the Materia Medica is so generally used, without the aid of a physician, as alcoholic stimulus; and the importance of a correct understanding of this one article by the people is beyond human ability to estimate. Intelligent humanity do not run into depravity willingly, with their eyes open; they are, too frequently, the victims of intellectual blindness — more to be pitied than despised. It is easy to comprehend the powerful influence of education, involved in urging onward the practice of stimulation, in the belief that our jaded powers can receive new accessions of power from alcoholic stimulus.

It is plain that the best applied remedy for intemperance consists in correcting our intellectual influences; here is the basis for the strongest appeal that ever moved the impulses of a nation, impressing a conviction of duty superior to all other means ever brought to bear on this question.

Intellect rules the world; not tyranny. Ideas give direction to national and individual customs; and this doctrine of power, or the opposite, in alcoholic mixtures, is significant, for good or for evil, in accordance with the belief of the people.

FERRI. — IRON.

In conformity with the provisions of a certain law, the ultimate elements must be carried though a vegetable process previous to being assimilated; but the law is very generally waived *in opinion*, in relation to the subject of iron. We are taught by our standard books, and from the chair professional, that chemically prepared compounds of iron are food. How shall we solve this seeming contradiction? It is unquestioned that iron is an important and natural constituent of the blood, for it enters into the formation of a certain organized body in the blood. Also, in anæmic or bloodless patients, the administration of iron chemically prepared seems, and in fact does, occasion an augmented supply of blood, often followed by a restoration of health to the patient.

Putting these two facts together, it is not difficult to persuade ourselves that the mentioned law does not prove true in relation to iron, which seems to be assimilated by the vital powers as it comes from the hand of the chemist.

With this encouraging precedent of belief in assimilation, various other seemingly required elements of the human organism are offered to the vital powers in a form given by the chemist, with a view to assimilation.

Small primary errors lead us onward to the committal of a practice which is supported by certain theories and contraindicated and contradicted by other theories; therefore, starting off with the theory that elements from the hands of the chemist can be assimilated, how far can we proceed before we find ourselves entangled in a manner which seems both consistent and inconsistent.

How far is this law waived in relation to such assimilation? Does it include iron only, or where does it stop? It must stop somewhere, or we shall be drawing our nourishment from chemical compounds instead of vegetable productions.

I trust the reader can see where this theory of the assimilation of chemical compounds will lead us in practice, and it becomes us to pause, and inquire if we have not been persuaded by theory to an errōneous practice in this direction, with chemical compounds.

The law which determines whether a substance is food or otherwise, has been alluded to, and in support of this applied law we all comprehend that the material substance required to be vitalized, to become a part of the human structure proper, must become fixed (as the chemists say) in that compound of living humanity, and perform the functions of its purpose, and be disintegrated after the manner of worn-out tissues; otherwise it has not been food to that organization into whose system it has been introduced, absorbed, and expelled.

A certain substance may fulfill a very important requirement in our organic system as a medicine; for instance, the acid contents of the intestines, in some cases of diarrhœa, may cause irritation and further continuance of the disease, and by a free use of alkalies the acidity is neutralized, and the disease cured. Alkalies, thus introduced, are not food, nor assimilated, although absorption and elimination takes place; and yet soda is a constituent element of the human organization. Not long since, an article appeared in a medical journal, which theorized that alkalies were food under such circumstances.

Certain elements in food are natural constituents of the human organism, and, in order to be assimilated, must be presented in that form which vegetation has modified; and iron is one of those elements which vegetative power lifts up, as it were, to a condition which renders it susceptible of assimilation by the vital processes of animal life.

The average amount of iron in the human system is about thirty-one grains, and it can be traced no further in organization than a constituent of the blood corpuscles. A corpuscle minus its iron is of little or no use, and can scarcely be said to be a corpuscle. The function fulfilled by the iron in the corpuscles seems to be that of an oxygen carrier. The iron of the corpuscle absorbs oxygen from the atmospheric air in the lungs, and returns to the heart and general capillary circulation as a peroxide of iron (that is, the largest amount possible to carry), and yields it up for a certain purpose, and then returns to the heart and lungs as a protoxide of iron, and again takes another supply, and thus continues to repeat the operation *ad infinitum*.

How long the *same* iron will continue to fulfill this function has never been determined, although it is very evident that it does fulfill this function for a long period, without any sensible appreciation or diminution, or known supply through the food, although, perhaps, our means of detecting iron in food are not so positive as of other substances. It is evident that iron thus obtained is food, but this is not evidence that iron from the hands of the chemist is food, although it may be useful and indispensable. Soluble iron is readily absorbed by the stomach when acid is present, furnished by the gastric secretion, although only in very small quantities, and unites with the red globules or corpuscles of the blood, and exists as free iron, but is not assimilated, and is soon eliminated by the kidneys. Iron thus introduced fulfills a temporary use in the corpuscle, and is soon eliminated, and its continued use must be maintained in order to restore those conditions which a proper quantity only, can maintain.

If the iron thus supplied becomes food, if it is assimilated as is iron from the vegetative supply, it would not be necessary to continue its prolonged use; and the very fact that it must be thus continued is evidence that it is not fixed by assimilation, but subserves only a temporary use of much less duration than when otherwise supplied.

A certain proportion of red corpuscles in the blood become as necessary for the continuance of health as the relative proportion of atmospheric air to the required wants of respiration; and, with a certain class of anæmic patients, the relative proportion of red corpuscles is lacking only from a want of iron [that is not true with all cases], and the iron thus artificially supplied subserves the *temporary* purpose of increasing the supply of red corpuscles in a given quantity of the blood, sometimes from forty to one hundred and sixty. In this manner only is iron subservient to convalescence; it favors the augmentation of the corpuscles, which, in fulfillment of this function, carry the requisite amount of oxygen.

Supposing we have under treatment one of those cases of anæmia, requiring more blood from increased corpuscle, and more corpuscles from a supply of iron, and the theory as here advocated is true, how are we to account for that time coming when we can discontinue the use of iron with this patient?

If the iron thus supplied is only temporary, and is soon eliminated, how are we to explain the permanency of the relative proportion of red corpuscles after artificial iron is eliminated? It may be proper to illustrate this by approximate analogy. In the case of a dyspeptic, a proper amount and kind of food is supplied, but the amount of the elaborated digestive fluids are not sufficient to enable the execution or perfection of assimilation. Thus the system suffers from the want of nourishment, although the material is present which furnishes it. The artificial use of pepsine, pancreatine, and lacto-peptine, assists digestion and admits of a larger quantity of food being assimilated, which, in fulfillment of its required use, augments the supply of these digestive fluids, and, sooner or later, those processes are self-sustaining and supplying.

In the supply of iron, something analogous to this seems rational; the anæmic patient has not the ability to assimilate the iron from the vegetable food; the organic power cannot reinstate or fix the proper supply from the nutritive source, consequently, the artificial supply for temporary use increases the number of the corpuscles, and quantity of blood, for the time, through which the harmonious action of vital ability, sooner or later, becomes self-sustaining.

The red corpuscle is formed by differentiation, or process of development, through the agency of the lymphatics; thus the lymph corpuscle eventually becomes the red corpuscle of the blood; and through some defective ability, perhaps not within our limits of comprehension, the corpuscle is imperfectly elaborated, the iron is not present, or not fixed, in accordance with assimilation, and a deficiency in the blood constitutes anæmia. The absorption of the iron chemically prepared, fulfills the completion of the elaborated corpuscle to the extent of temporary usefulness only; therefore the iron is not assimilated, consequently is not food; yet it is absorbed, and fulfills the temporary use of an oxygen carrier, and is eliminated as free iron, not as disintegrated tissue.

PHOSPHORUS.

The doctrine that iron is food, and is assimilated from those preparations in medicinal use, has paved the way for a belief in and introduction of phosphorus, not only as a medicine, but as a supply to nerve tissue; and in illustration of the manner of introducing this substance to the profession, allow me to quote from reputed acceptable authority as follows: —

" I claim for phosphorus, duly administered and properly exhibited — and for this purpose I advocate its employment in its elementary form in an absolute state of subdivision, and in thoroughly protected *pill* shape — more specific powers in certain and constantly recurring maladies than opium, quinine, calomel, or cod-liver oil can claim. From personal experience, and from the experience of others, I would state that, whereas we can readily find substitutes for the remedies above in almost any case in which they may be demanded, yet, in no one instance, can we supplement phosphorus when *it* is indicated. In cases where phosphorus is demanded, where, in the extended range of Materia Medica, can we look for a remedy which will substitute that potent agent. As phosphorus enters largely into the composition of the human structure, especially of the nervous system, with its great centre, it has long been thought that in case of wear and tear of body and brain, phosphorus could be wisely administered to repair waste. Certain diets containing phosphorus, have for a long time been popular with practitioners of comprehensive views, and in cases of *over work*, of *mental exhaustion*, *mania*, and *impotency*, have acted wonderfully well."

We are thus instructed that phosphorus from both sources becomes food, and also that in the elementary state it has specific powers, and in a fish diet acts wonderfully well. *Vide*, " Professor Agassiz laid special stress on fish diet where the brain had been tasked and taxed beyond its capacity. It is only natural to credit any benefit derived to the phosphorus element which abounds in fish, which element goes to the repair of waste tissue in the brain. Taking it for granted that this beneficial repairing effect *is* due to phosphorus in the fish diet, the question naturally arises, why cannot the exhibition of phosphorus itself be resorted to, either in lieu of the fish diet, or as a powerful adjunct in connection with it ?

Such an addition would most assuredly hasten the cure, especially where brain exhaustion is produced."

There is no mistaking the lack of analysis of thought on this subject.

Vide, " There is one reason why the exhibition of phosphorus in certain diseases has not been resorted to by physicians. That reason is, *fear* of the remedy. I do inveigh against needless timidity in the use of the remedy which, even were it pushed too far, could be rendered powerless by an emetic dose of tartarized antimony and potassa, and a drachm of magnesia suspended in a glass of water."

Allow me to wonder whether the phosphorus remains in the alimentary canal, and, like a king on his throne, exercises his *power.* If so, how can it contribute to the supply of the brain as a tissue? If it does so contribute to the brain, does the emetic and purgative *power,* which renders phosphorus " powerless," drive it out of the brain? Or does the antimony and magnesia coax or draw it back into said canal and vomit it up or purge it down? This is merely query. *Vide,* " That phosphorus is a speedy and powerful *nerve tonic* there is ample testimony, — Dr. Routh, of London, being especially loud in its praise. And, in addition to the administration of phosphorus, he, along with other directions, is earnest that the patient should have a nourishing diet, especially of shell fish. Concerning the rationale (explanation) of the action of phosphorus, it is but frank and honest on our part to say, that as yet, with our present light before us, we cannot satisfactorily explain it. ' But,' using the words of an eminent authority, ' probably the progress of animal chemistry will hereafter supply the missing links now wanting to connect the phosphorus taken as a medicine with the protagon of the brain, and then with the phosphates which are finally thrown off by the body.'

" The popular idea, that as phosphorus is found in the nervous structure generally, so a beneficial result may be achieved by supplying this same element to the weakened structure, will not on a crucial test hold good. For instance, we might with equal consistency and reason attempt to live on charcoal, because carbon is a constituent of the tissues."

All of these quotations are from the same author except quotations within a quotation; the author has labored hard to persuade us to believe what he afterwards says is impossible to be true, namely, that an element as such, can be a food. This cannot be, even when it may become a constituent of our organization subsequent to vegetative organization. When the " crucial test " is made the theory does not hold good, yet like the one whom he quotes, he thinks animal chemistry will supply the missing link which connects the phosphorus as a medicine with the protagon of the brain ; but confesses that he does not know much about it, which he thinks it " honest to say."

What is the lesson taught? We are instructed that the element phosphorus is good to supply waste brain ; also, that it is impossible to thus supply waste tissue. What is the persuasive drift, or tendency, or practical action, intended or advised, on this subject of phosphorus, by this writer? In conclusion, we are instructed to practice with the expectation of a result, in accordance with the former theory, that it does supply the waste tissue of the system; and the article closes thus: "This paper is respectfully laid before the profession in the sole and sincere hope that phosphorus, such a powerful agent, may be assigned a higher and nobler place in therapeutic art, than for years it has been holding. I do affirm, from the teachings of the best of teachers, *experience*, that in certain affections it is beyond value and without an equal."

Such dissertations plentifully abound in medical literature, in the expounding of science, with the science left out.

In support of such a conclusion, we are not alone asked to be persuaded by his theory, but it is due to "the best of teachers, *experience*," that we be convinced of its unequaled value. Reference is made to "practitioners of comprehensive views," whose experience not only gives weight to their convictions, but should, he thinks, entail upon us similar belief, who speak highly of phosphorus when supplied in a fish diet; and Dr. Routh, of London, whose name is mentioned, "is *earnest* that the patient should have a nourishing diet, especially of shell fish." Dr. Routh and Agassiz recommend organized phosphorus, only; they have not committed themselves or given any support to the doctrine that phosphorus from the hand of the chemist is assimilable.

Such unreasonable contradictory theories and assertions are not rare, but very numerous; yet they do not indicate a second-rate brain, for so long as medical men are taught and do believe the medical power theory, they cannot give expression to their views otherwise than in this contradictory manner.

When any subject is explored with a conformity to the

medical power theory, it is sure to give the lie to the physiological and vital theory, and the reverse. We cannot believe in both, and be consistent in our philosophy; either the vital theory or the medical power theory must be surrendered, for correct explanations of the laws of nature are not antagonistic; and these theories are positively in opposition.

TONICS.

Direct tonics are food; medicinal tonics do not impart to the organisms any power, nor add to the sum total of vital power; their use consists in occasioning a change of manifestation of vital power, which change is more favorable to harmonious balanced nutritive accumulation.

POISON.

Poisons belong to the same division of material as medicines, the presence of which in the human system are very detrimental to harmonious vital action, and will occasion a special vital disturbance sufficient to cause death. My opponents in theory claim that poisons are possessed of so much *power* as to nearly or quite destroy the organism.

The line of demarkation established by medical power theorists, between a medicine and a poison, is one of accumulated or inherent power. Thus a small quantity of power in a substance allows it to be classified as a medicine; a larger quantity of power, occasions it to be called a poison.

The quantity of a medicine may be increased sufficient to occasion toxilogical effects, or a poison may be so diluted, that a small amount may occasion only what is termed a medicinal effect.

The word "poison" is associated with an idea of *power*, and we have been educated to retain this association for centuries; yet it is false.

A poison is a substance the presence of which occasions such violent disturbance of vital action as to endanger and often cause death.

There is no natural law or dividing line between a medicine, as the term is generally used, and a poison, although practically there is an essential difference in result between a medicinal or a poisonous dose.

FACTS.

It is well known that those persons who are possessed of a hardy, vigorous constitution, capable of enduring much beyond the average of the human race, whenever they are afflicted with acute disease, are thought to be, and they are in fact, more in danger of dying, than those of weak and feeble constitutions. Why is this?

Does the *same cause* which makes *them* sick possess more power when taken into their system than it possesses when taken into the system of the more enfeebled?

If the cause of a disease is possessed of a power which acts on the human organism, why does this power act so violently in strong constitutions? This one fact alone is sufficient to cause the whole medical profession to see the error of the assumed power theory in medicine and poison, if they were not blinded by this inherited belief.

Persons afflicted with chronic maladies are less liable to acute sickness; and a previously enfeebled person will live through a sickness which is astonishing, if you were to believe that the power which perverts those actions was inherent in the *cause*.

Merely reverse the theory of the source of power, and that class of patients are then reasonably presumed to avoid death from having less of those vigorous actions which destroy special organs or develop high temperatures; and it becomes a question of prolonged endurance, whether vital power is to become exhausted, and death follow; or there is to be a prolonged prostration and recovery.

The vigorous patient seldom dies of exhaustion of vital power, but the vigorous action destroys some organ or develops a temperature too high for the restoration of a balanced nerve influence, which reminds us of the great importance of keeping the temperature down in acute diseases.

Surgeons are familiar with some of these facts, not by theory alone, but by actual observation, and they are made subservient to success in capital operations. The probabilities of recovery in ovarian disease are much more favorable if the general system begins to wane before the tumor is removed. The danger after such an operation is often through inflammatory action, and if the vital powers are previously enfeebled, this action is of less degree. Again, the philosophy of the use of a stimulus in such operation is very much involved in that fact, that the vital powers are otherwise engaged; that is, the amount of vital energy thus deployed detracts from what would, otherwise, be fully manifested; and it is thus deployed in a more diffusable manner with less relative local injury.

This same application can be made to many of those cases of rattlesnake poison which recover by the free use of a stimulus.

The same principle of dividing up vital activity is exhibited in the use of the blister.

The more minutely this one power or vital theory is applied to the explanation of the varied manifestations of disease, and effects of medicine, the more apparent, harmonious, and convincing will the theory become; and it will be realized that a science, with a theory which explains the laws of those manifestations involved in the elements of the science, in its practical workings, is worthy of a name much unlike that expressed by Dr. John Mason Good, "The language of medical science is a barbarous jargon."

Says Dr. Evans, F. R. C., of London, "The popular medical system has neither philosophy nor common sense to commend it to confidence."

I have long maintained a great contempt for our medical philosophy, but it is practically wise not to condemn a principle without superseding it with a better substitute.

SUMMARY.

PHYSIOLOGICAL action is vital action in relation to usable material.

PATHOLOGICAL action is vital action in relation to undigestible, effete, and foreign material.

MEDICINAL action is a misnomer. Medicinal effect expresses the fact without a violation of a principle in science.

POISONOUS action is also a misnomer; it should be poisonous effect.

PHYSIOLOGICAL experiments with drugs, and physiological action of drugs: this is a very unscientific and perverted use of languague, and conveys the idea that physiological functions are executed by the supposed *power* in medicines, instead of vital power.

ACTIVE *principle*, in medicine, should be called " medicinal portion."

MEDICINAL *property* is a misnomer; it should be " medicinal relation; " medicine has no properties except physical, such as relate to material in general.

REFLEX ACTION, conveys the idea that there has been a previous action, which is not correct; there has been a sensation previous to the action, but sensation is not action; consequently, what is called a reflex action is a primary action. The problem is expressed thus: cause, sensation — instinctive volition or action. It would more nearly approximate the true expression of the principles of the science, to substitute the term " reflex operations " for " reflex action."

SENSATION pertains to contact, or recognition at insensible distances.

SENSIBILITY is a brain function of recognition, regardless of distance. Our sensibility may be aware of the disagreeable sensation of a part, but the part is not possessed of acute sensibility.

Medicine and poison have no associated power inherent to the substance.

The cause of disease has no inherent power. All power which gives motion to vitalized structures is vital power. The greatest error ever perpetrated by the mind in relation to the human organism, consists in the doctrine that there are *inherent powers* in inorganic matter, which give motion to, or act on living tissues.

The practical science of medicine consists in controlling the instinctive organic power by the use of medicine as a *cause*, which occasions this power to manifest itself in accordance with the best interest of the individual, when properly prescribed.

A theory of medical science or disease, based on the interpretation that there is a power in medicine or poison which acts on the living human organism in any possible manner, is as absurd and contradictory to the laws of science, as the ancient fallacious doctrines, that the earth was the centre of the solar system.

I submit the foregoing premises to the criticisms of an intelligent profession, with a full belief that my interpretation is generally correct; and trust that, sooner or later, the principles here inculcated will be adopted as a guide in the practice of medicine, and be indoctrinated from the chair professional.

These principles are important, both for the development of a science, and the protection of the people from the national curse, quackery; thereby inculcating a rational belief that none but those schooled in the principles of the science, can safely prescribe for the controlling of that instinctive vital force which develops and perfects the human organisms; and likewise as involving the greatest questions which affect the welfare of a nation.

PART SECOND.

DIFFERENT SYSTEMS OF PRACTICE.

WHAT has been said relative to the inconsistency of medical philosophy in Part First, is directly applicable to the regular system of medical philosophy, and those who are slow to make an application of a principle to science, may infer that some other systems are nearer perfection, and better adapted to meet the requirements of humanity, should we neglect to assign them their position in the scale of merit. Of the various systems there is nothing in particular to engage our attention except homœopathy, unlike what belongs to the regular, except that some schools prefer to select their medicines from the vegetable kingdom, on the plea that they are more sanative and less poisonous; such a pretext is only an expression of credulity, distinguished by a great lack of knowledge relative to the creation of vegetable poisons. In the vegetable kingdom are found Hyoscyamus, Conium maculatum, Aconite, Belladonna, Strychnia, without mentioning a score of lesser ones; thus the vegetable kingdom far excels the mineral in the production of poisons. While others claim to have superior abilities in making their selections of medicine, and choose only those which have well disposed and peaceable powers, that are always willing to do good, without any of those malicious inclinations to do harm, and that they select from each system all the good and reject the bad. This is beautiful in idea, and thus it ends.

HOMŒOPATHY.

This is the modern intellectual race horse, competing for the fame of science. Its founders and promulgators are entitled to the credit of an ingenious originality of thought which far surpasses in transcendent absurdity anything which has ever been submitted for the consideration of an intelligent public. They strike out boldly in their text-books and literature, by declaring that, " the supremacy of medicine is a matter of vast importance ; problems of the deepest interest await for solution the development of that science."

With this undisguised acknowledgment that the light of science is not sufficiently developed to illuminate those " problems of deepest interest," and while very restive with this insurmountable barrier or deep chasm between their acquired abilities and the open field of science, rich in its created blessings, they have seen fit to bridge this chasm, which has long kept back and out the human mind from those richest treasures ; not that we may pass over and up to science, but that science may come over and down to us.

Not being able to move man up to the science, they propose to move the science down to man, take it across the chasm, and simplify it to man's understanding, reset its profundities with principles of simplicity on a level with the diminutive mind, and thus harmonize the science so "that its principles from their explicitness and simplicity are better fitted for the popular understanding."

The special distinction which they covet, separating themselves from all other schools of philosophy, consists, not in rejecting the belief of an *inherent power* in drugs, *but that this power, instead of acting on vitalized structure on its own responsibility*, has an *affinity* for *vital powers*, and *unites* with them in the coöperative duty, or correlation of force, to execute activities or vital manifestations.

Before we proceed, let us inquire into the meaning of the term "affinity" and acquire a perfect understanding of all that the term implies, and its applications in the English language.

This is a pivotal term, a knowledge of which gives inclination to ideas; its most specific application is expressed in Chemical Science, when two different elements at insensible distances, like oxygen and hydrogen, unite to form water, a compound body, the physical character of which is very much unlike either of the separate elements; the law which expresses this possibility of union, is called the law of affinity. The term is used in social science, to express a similarity of mental sentiment, or conformity; more particularly as a comparative expression. What can affinity mean when applied to the Science of Medicine? Its application is not with the thought that medical power and vital power unite and form a different power, but is used in a supposed relative sense on the baseless supposition that there are a thousand or more varieties of vital power, which act specifically on particular structures; also that there are a thousand or more varieties of medical powers, which are endowed with specific abilities to *act* on the *same* particular structure; therefore, the kind of *medical power* which they say was intended to act on any particular structure, is said to have an affinity for the *vital power* which was ordained to take charge of this particular part; thus, the two powers go into partnership and act similia similibus, constituting the invention which they call *affinity* or law of *specifics*. This is the principle whose "explicitness is simplified and fitted for the popular understanding," and is the most gigantic error of modern intellectual man. This school claims that the more a medicine is diluted, the greater are its curative powers. And the practitioner of this simplified science is required to prescribe by the law of *affinity* and administer the *specific medicine*, which affiliates with the particular vital power involved in the trouble; which prescriptions are illustrated by the table of remedies for toothache, copied from the "Homœopathic Practice of Medicine" by Dr. M. Freligh, visiting Physician to the New York Homœopathic Dispensary Association, and member of the Hahnemann Academy of Medicine.

Pages 170, 171.

For toothache, especially from cold . . . . . *Aconite.*
For violent tearing in the teeth of the lower jaw . *Agaricus.*
For dull drawing in the upper and right row of teeth all night . . . . *Belladonna.*
For toothache caused by either hot or cold things . . . *Calcarea-Carb.*
For toothache aggravated by warm drinks . . . *Cham.*
For throbbing toothache . . . . *China.*
For jerking toothache . . . . *Hepar-Sulph.*

DIFFERENT SYSTEMS OF PRACTICE. 109

For toothache only when eating . . . . . *Kali-Carb.*
For lacerating, tearing toothache (Rattle-snake Virus) . . *Lachesis.*
For toothache only at night . . . . *Mercurius.*
For toothache occurring after dinner . . . *Nux Vomica.*
For toothache with swelling of the cheek . . *Phosphorus.*
For toothache aggravated by taking anything warm into the mouth . . . . *Pulsatilla.*
For drawing toothache extending to the ear . . . *Sepia.*
For throbbing, lacerating toothache aggravated by cold water . . . . *Spigelia.*
For toothache caused by draft of air . . . . . *Sulphur.*
For toothache during pregnancy . . . . . . *Sepia.*
For toothache relieved by cold drinks . *Bryonia, Pulsatilla.*
For toothache relieved by warm drinks . *Lycopod, Sulph.*
For toothache relieved by smoking . . . . . *Mercury.*
For toothache aggravated by smoking . *Ignatia, Bryonia.*
For toothache relieved by warmth . *Merc., Nox Vom., Sulph.*

The professors say the simplicity of this science, "is its best eulogy, for enlightened adoption by all classes in nearly all parts of the civilized world." I also quote from the revised edition of "Medical Philosophy," 1875, by D. A. Gorton, M. D., an able expounder of Homœopathy, and a shining light, page 28: "It is well known that particular drugs produce specific psychical effects, either virtuous or vicious, morally strengthening or depressing, by virtue of the selective affinity which they possess, for particular parts of the brain or nervous centres — and they thus have the power to modify the functions of the part acted upon. Who among close observers of medicinal actions does not know the efficacy of Sulphur in obstinate contumacy; of Chamomile in a fretful, peevish disposition; of Belladonna in certain forms of " temper disease; " of Anacardium Orientalis in cruelty and profanity; of Hyoscyamus in jealousy; of Nux Vomica in maliciousness; of Stramonia in cowardice." Page 30, *vide*. "There is not a single operative medicine [says Hahnemann] that does not effect a notable change in the temper and manner of thinking." Page 36, *vide*. "I declare, on the basis of my experience in the medicinal treatment of moral maladies, my confidence in sulphur as a remedy for sin, original or acquired. Common salt is certainly one of nature's great sin detergents and moral prophylactics," *vide* page 53. "My own predilections lie in the direction of a rigid individualization of every disease, and its remedy; of a small, but not the smallest dose, and of a fair trial with a single remedy." This author claims to have made some advancement over his fellow professionals, and he defines himself thus, on page 58: "Rotten tonsils and carious teeth have been treated for weeks and months, by over scrupulous homœopathists, with medicated pellets, when the true indication was the forceps and bistoury." Again on page 60, "Another colleague had a pet remedy in Thuja Occidentalis. It was said to cure Variola (smallpox) so quickly in his hands that the pustules had not time to mature." Page 61, *vide*. "Among the eighty or more homœopathic physicians in Brooklyn, I doubt if there could be found twenty — probably not ten — capable of rendering in a chronic disease, or in an acute case, if obscure, a sound prescription according to the law of similars." Notwithstanding the simplicity which recommends this practice to the people, this author seems to have a very poor idea of the intellectual proficiency of his fellow practitioners in Brooklyn, N. Y.

Hahnemann, the central star in this constellation of nonsense, and father of this large progeny, says in his "Organon of Medicine," as mentioned on page 70 by same author: "Homœopathy sheds not a drop of blood, administers no emetics, purgatives, laxatives, or diaphoretics — never subdues pain by opium."

In Freligh's "Practice of Medicine," pages 26–28, we are informed that the duration of action of these infinitesimal doses of medicine are as follows: —

The power in Arnica acts from six to ten days.
Borax acts six weeks.
Animal charcoal acts about forty days.
Vegetable charcoal acts forty days.
Coffee acts about ten days.
Lachesis acts from four to five weeks.
Rhubarb acts from one to ten days.
Sulphur acts from six days to two and three weeks.

To further illustrate the application of the infinitesimal dose, with its augmented special powers, I will copy from the same author the results of philosophical deduction, of the various remedies specifically indicated by affinity for the treatment of inflammation of the brain.

Pages 73, 74.

When the heat of the head is great, face flushed and bloated . . . . *Belladonna.*
When there is loss of consciousness, the patient raving at times . . . . *Hyoscyamus.*
When the face is red; eyes not much injected, but rather bright . . . . *Stramonia.*

When the pains in the head are shooting, and aggravate by motion . . . . *Bryonia.*
When the patient remains in a comatose state as if sleeping from the effects of an anodyne . . . . *Opium.*
When caused by intestinal irritation, as worms . . . . . *Aconite and Belladonna.*
When caused by teething. After *Aconite* and *Belladonna* give *Cham.*
When caused by a blow. *Arnica* must be given first, then other drugs.

Page 112, *vide.*

" For inflammation of the knee. When the pain is violent, with tremulousness of the knees . . . . *Belladonna.*
When the pain is tensive, and increased by motion *Bryonia.*
When the pain is dull and worse at night . . . *Rhus-tox.*
When the pain is of a stiffening character . . . *Sulphur.*
When the pain is gnawing, lacerating . . . . *Mercurius.*
When caused by a bruise. *Arnica,* external."

Page 295, *vide.*

" For Hernia, (rupture). Among the remedies that have been successfully employed in the case of Hernia, are *Aconite, Aurum, Cocculus, Lycopodium, Nux Vomica, Silicea, Nitric Acid, Sulphur, Opium, Arnica, Rhus-tox* and *Sul. acid.* If symptoms of gangrene set in, *Lachesis, Arsenic.*"

Page 460, 462.

" For falling off of the hair. When it is caused by grief, *Phos. Acid, Staphysagria.* When caused by severe attacks of headache, *Hepar Sulph., Nitric Acid, Antimony, Silex* (Sand), *Sepia, Sulph.* When the hair falls off from the sides of the head. *Graphites* (black lead), *Phosphorus, Kali-Carb.*
When from the fore part of the head . *Arsenicum, Natrum.*

When from the back part of the head . . . .
Vegetable Charcoal and *Silex.*
When from the temples . . . . *Calc, Kali, Lycopodium.*
When from spots or different parts of the head . . . . .
Cantharis (Spanish flies) *Phosphorus, Iodine.*
When falling out of the whiskers, *Calc-Carb., Graphites* (black lead), and *Natrum-Muriat.* (common salt).

" First administer the remedy directed by the cause, two or more doses, as may be required, after which the condition of the hair and scalp should direct the remedy. one dose a day or every second day. Diet in accordance with homœopathic rules."

If homœopathic *philosophy* is such superlative nonsense as here represented, which we must all admit, how are we to reconcile it with the success which so frequently attends the sick when thus treated?

We are to bear in mind that disease is vital action in relation to obnoxious or non-usable material, and the pathological or diseased action manifested is divided in Part First, thus: one class of actions require to be understood and let alone, for the vital power is doing the best for the recovery of the patient that is possible to be executed. With this kind of disease homœopathic treatment, or any kind of applied simplicity, or let-alone-ativness, will not interfere with the success of the patient, and will furnish apparent reason, with those who do not comprehend the principle involved in the cure, to glorify this wonderful modern invention.

The other division of pathological or diseased action, is mentioned as being that kind of action which is acting very unwisely, and requires to be medicated for the purpose of guiding it into different activities, for the better interests of the patient. We may inquire, how does homœopathic treatment meet the requirements of this class of maladies? We reply, that it has no more effect on this class of disturbances than moral suasion, although as an observer you may be induced to believe otherwise, for a proper dose, such as is used by the "regulars" may be prepared in a concentrated form and not seem to violate the rules deduced by this modern philosophy, or tarnish the flag of the system, which is waved with much briskness to inspire the patient in the belief that there has been no change of philosophic base carried into practice.

The practitioner of Homœopathy may prescribe remedies properly and possess that requisite good sense implied in the correct interpretation of events, and we are aware of some excellent practitioners who do business under that name. This rebuke of homœopathic philosophy is not an attack on the personal merit and skill of any individual, of the many known members of the school. It is against homœopathic philosophy, theoretical and applied, that we are contending, not the man himself. Therefore, to convince the reader that there is a great departure by this school of practitioners, I will quote from the distinguished Dr. Gorton, in his Revised "Medical Philosophy," page 49, commencing with the last line: "The new or Homœopathic school has been unhappily divided into a trinity of medical sects: the low dilutionists, the high dilutionists, the medium dilutionists; and the old dogmatic, partisan spirit is being kindled among them, and the love of truth which inspired the early homœopathists seems to have departed from his late followers. Surely Hahnemann, could he speak, would rebuke in no uncertain tones these latter day dogmatists."

Thus entrenched by this authority, we are supported in saying, that there is a great departure in practice from what is advised through the deductions of homœopathic philosophy.

The practical inadequateness of this system to fulfill the dictates of common sense which has ever been the great antagonist to this practice, has occasioned the more advanced thinkers of this school to adopt the ways of the regular physician. Thus those practical come-outers, whose common sense is superior to their previous indoctrinated philosophy, have learned by experience that a certain class of disturbed actions require to be altered and modified by larger doses of medicine, instead of supplying that kind of medicine which occasions vital force to exert more energy in the direction which was previously manifested on the plan of similars or supposed affinity.

In conclusion, it is not difficult to discover how the idea or belief in affinity of power, was born in the human mind. Hahnemann, like others, received by tradition and erroneous culture the belief in a medical power; and not understanding the relation of material to vital force, on the plan that certain articles do not occasion a change of vital action except in large doses, and not observing any opposite effect from the administration of a medicine in a certain small dose, the inference was that this power introduced must do something; therefore, it was very presumable that it might have an affinity for the resident vital power, and united with it to further augment the diseased action being manifested. Together with the above, also, is the fact that he did not know that vital force or power could and did act pathologically, both wise and unwise, with a view to self-preservation; and recognizing the former only, he thought every pathological action must be accelerated and aided; thus, with these important facts completely outside of his comprehension, both of the plan of relation between material and vital force, and pathological action being manifested both wise and unwise, he invented the theory that the two kinds of power, medical and vital, should have an affinity to unite and augment the then existing disturbed action, with a view to thus restore a harmonious physiological action, or health, sooner or later. This was equivalent to admitting that the diseased action was always directed intelligently instead of by an instinct, which might be either wise or unwise, and the doctrine of similars or affinity of powers, was presented for the acceptance of a non-comprehensive public in the name of *similia similibus curantur*, or homœopathy.

Practically, the homœopathic theory does not provide for sufficient medicine in many cases, while the "regular" provides for too much in many cases. Nature has provided but one law of cure, and one code of principles to be observed in the treatment of disease, and whenever the law of vital force is indoctrinated correctly, all medical philosophy will be alike, and but one school of medicine will be recognized by the interpreters of science.

THE PRESENT STATE OF MEDICAL SCIENCE.

Organic matter has an activity given to itself which it must display; and the doctrine of physiology is the statement of the various developments accomplished with organic matter by the vital force, in the normal exercise of its powers. Physiological science has advanced to a position, which is very acceptable in its representation of the law, in fulfilling its primary duties of developing and maintaining the human organism.

The phenomena are studied, with a view to explain physiology, as an expression inherent to vital force, and the success of this inquiry is evidence of a sufficient mental ability to cope with the mysteries of our existence, when furnished with a correct basis or true principle in nature, from which to reason.

The result of our success in this direction contrasts strangely with the result of our efforts in endeavoring to explain pathological processes.

Physiological actions are studied from the correct supposition that they are executed by the inherent powers in our system, while pathological actions are studied from the erroneous supposition that they are executed by a power not vital, but a power foreign to our vitalized tissues and inherent in effete matter and poison.

One is crowned with a universal acknowledgment of success, and the other an inconsistent jargon of opinions. When ancient man lifted his portals to give comprehensive range to his intellect, and sought to bring his thoughts into unison with those of the Creator, and viewed humanity, so wonderfully made, he fell short of his ambition.

He did not recover the true interpretation of the vital principle, but accounted for various actions in the human system, as being due to powers entirely foreign to our existence.

What should have been the recovery of the ideal prototype of God's plan, was a blank; he could not comprehend man, so mysteriously made, but adopted in part a substitute by drawing an ideal plan, that man was created in substance in a manner which enabled his organs to execute normal activities by virtue of a vital principle, while the abnormal activities of the same organs were supposed to be moved, accelerated, retarded, or altered by a power inherent to some other material.

He could not comprehend how the vital principle could have two sets of laws; one its law and harmony of action in relation to the usable material, and the other a law of abnormal action in relation to material not usable.

Our schools to-day are indoctrinating the same ancient interpretation of two kinds of powers, which run the machinery of human life, and I am almost persuaded to say they are doing worse, for our medical books abound in records of powers, inherent to inorganic matter, which have the ability to execute physiological actions.

From a certain catalogue of a medical school of the first order, I quote: "Therapeutics, or the physiological action of drugs and their application to disease, are taught in the third year by lecture." This is not a solitary instance of this kind of theorizing; but such theory is on the increase in our medical literature.

Of a very recent date in one of our substantial medical journals is an article entitled, "The Physiological Action of Thebain," giving an account of "physiological experiments with Thebain," and it appears that a great proportion of the experiments proved fatal to the lower animals.

It was found that the physiological action of Thebain would cause convulsions quicker than either of five other alkaloids, and rigor mortis quickly ensue. This is a curious idea, to have physiological action cause death, except by senility. We are likewise informed that in opium are found "seventeen alkaloids and two organic acids," and human ingenuity has endowed the drug opium with about twenty different kinds of powers, in order to be consistent with the theory which is supported only by appearances.

This kind of literature is very prevalent in our schools and books, and becomes a constituent of our mongrel education, and how long we are to continue the pursuit of this inconsistent medley, remains problematical.

Says Dr. Brown-Sequard in referring to certain errors, " Physicians, unfortunately, I speak of myself as well as of others, are biased. This bias prevents progress. They have received an education which has given them certain notions, and those notions prevent a free examination of certain questions."

Bacon says, " Not only what was asserted once is asserted still, but what were questions once are questions still, and, instead of being resolved by discussion, are only fixed and fed." Are we creatures of tenacity ; stamped so indelibly by the court of custom, as to blot out our reason ?

The history of education, from the remotest period until quite recently, is in evidence, that when humanity manifested any peculiar freak, mentally, were insane or epileptic, it was thought that some foreign power had got into them, — the spirit of an animal, — or they were bewitched, or the evil one was in them. The educated have abolished those ideas, although the same principle is continued in relation to the effects occasioned by medicine; and those augmented mental powers, manifested by certain individuals, outside the general known law of mental perception, in a state of trance, are attributed by many to the power of a departed spirit, which has taken possession of the bodily organs, and is expressing a distinct individuality. It has always been a peculiar fact, that whenever the human mind could not comprehend human actions, the *cause* has been attributed to a foreign power, outside of our individual organic powers, or brain capabilities of perversion. The powers which have been given to mankind are great; and it is consistent to believe that by certain kinds of culture, we acquire abilities which transcend ordinary belief; and the time is not far distant when trance phenomena and the peculiar manifestations of the period will be reduced to certain principles in harmony with our individual living organization. Many of these principles are already within our reach, and others have a mental outline not far away. In relation to the nutrient material we call food, which has been lifted as it were from its elementary state, and organized by vegetative powers in such a manner that the animal life powers can seize and appropriate it for higher organizations, it is frequently the subject of erroneous thought, and very unscientifically defined; with some authors, different articles of food act on such and such parts of the human organism, and yield up their power.

Instead of entertaining the correct idea that an animal organism seizes the material by virtue of its own inherent powers, and so uses it that its own powers can continue to be manifested, the mind takes the deluded interpretation which the false medical power doctrine has inculcated, and theorizes that vital power is manifested by virtue of continued accessions or additions of power from food.

A certain writer defines food thus: "A food is that which, being innocent in relation to the tissues of the body, is a digestible or absorbable substance, that can be oxidized in the body and decomposed in such a way as to give up to the body the forces which it contains." Whatever portion of a material which is "oxidized" or "decomposed" is not convertible into tissue, or used in any of the constructive duties of organization, consequently is not food.

If the doctrine, that vital power is continued through the agency of continued accessions of power from other organizations or chemical compounds, is true, vitality would not be a special created principle, but a result.

The doctrines of our medical schools are based on the supposed laws of powers in two departments of nature. One, the law of vital power, the other, the law of medical power. Unfortunately for humanity and for science, our forefathers reasoned unwisely, and we are compelled out of pure respect to opinion, and nothing more, to persist in the attempt to explain our science from false premises. Consequently we hear the oft-repeated expression, "I do not think much of theories in medicine."

From the chair professional in regard to malarial poison we are taught that if vital power, or the powers of the system as they call it, succeed quickly in removing the cause of disease, and establish a balance, the phenomena can be considered as due to an effort of nature; but before the lecture is closed you will be instructed that if this disturbance is long continued the poisonous malaria takes on a morbid action, and exerts its powers on the liver and system generally.

Thus if a success is not readily accomplished by the vital power in removing the cause of fever and ague, the whole order and law of things are changed, a new power steps into activity. And to silence this second power we are instructed to introduce the third kind of a power found in quinine.

Dr. Brown-Sequard, of well known distinguished ability, attempts to establish the proofs of the supposed existence of a power in medicine under the following head: —

"POWER OF OXYGEN, STRYCHNINE, AND THE WILL."

"What now is the agent of production of nervous force in our blood? It is clear that blood itself must be necessary to the production of nerve force. Still, for a *time*,[1] the oxygen alone which is carried by the blood may suffice. Oxygen, even when the blood seems to have been taken away altogether from the part, can *give* some nerve *force* to the nervous system, but there is a medicinal agent which has immense *power* in producing nervous results.

[1] The italics in this quotation are mine.

"When the spinal cord of a frog has been washed of every drop of blood, when injections have been made of pure water so as to carry away every particle of blood, if strychnine is put on the spinal cord, in a very short time the amount of *reflex power*, which is a manifestation of nerve force, is very much greater than it was before, showing that strychnine has increased that power. This is the *only fact we know* which clearly proves that a medicine, putting aside oxygen, *can have such a power*, and a power, indeed, which is very great. . . . . What is the power of our will on the nerve force? This is a question which a great many patients every day ask themselves. There is no doubt that nerve force is very little under our will. It may be that we would spend it very foolishly, as we do spend many other things."

That part of the quotation after the " . . . . " is equivalent to admitting that there are two different sources from which life force is generated, namely, the voluntary and involuntary, or, in other words, the instinctive and the will power, which is in support of the theory of vitality advocated in the first part of this volume.

One simple fact, rightly understood and truly interpreted, will teach as much as a thousand facts of the same kind; thus the inductions which we get by observing the simple may be used with success to disentangle the phenomena of the complex, and to give a correct explanation to the phenomena introduced by Dr. Brown-Sequard in the application of strychnine to the spinal cord to prove the existence of a power in the strychnine. I will quote the same Dr. Brown-Sequard against himself: "There is an immense difference as regards the amount of nervous force that remains in the system after death, according to many circumstances, and especially according to temperature. If we have considerably diminished the temperature of animals having a great heat, such as we have, and we then kill them by means that will not bring on convulsions and an expenditure of force, we find that the amount of force that remains is considerable, and that it will remain there a very long time."

Now the kind of force which he refers to is the same as we witness when an eel is being cooked in the frying pan, if recently killed, the nerves of organic or instinctive force become irritated or surrounded with abnormal conditions affording sensations which occasion the writhing or contracting of the muscles. The heat in the cooking process occasions the muscular actions only while there is a remaining organic force; also in the application of the strychnine, those effects noticed are not prolonged beyond the time of the remaining organic force; thus Dr. Brown-Sequard furnishes us with the very principle which explains the phenomena, in regard to which he has made an erroneous interpretation. Therefore, the most positive and "only fact we know, which clearly proves that a medicine can have such a power," is completely reversed in its interpretation by a law of organic force illustrated by the same demonstrator.

This whole problem is plain enough when we learn that irritability of the nerve is not action of a foreign power on the nerve, but the action of its own organic power in relation to abnormal contact, or sensation, which, however, is a *cause*, but not a *power*.

Says Alexander Bain in his work on "Logic," when speaking of the ebb of intellectual acquirements: "The uncertainty where to look for the next opening of discovery brings the pain of conflict and the debility of indecision."

It seems worthy of consideration by the medical profession, and others who have the capacity and interest in the operations of science, to survey the fields of medical philosophy, and scan closely the relativity of phenomena. After your observation has taken in the facts, do not be content with the traditional philosophy which you have been educated to admire, against which your senses rebel; but go forth into the field of imagination for a trip of originality; search for principles which are in harmony with all *facts*.

Do not treat too lightly the idea of sending your imagination in pursuit of those primary principles, for it is through imagination that we acquire all of our most important knowledge, which imagination is corrected or confirmed by observation, and philosophy binds into one harmonious whole. It is through imagination that the greatest discoveries are made; imagination is but mental perception of non-tangible relations; our present medical philosophy is but deductions endeavoring to harmonize modern facts with ancient imagination. Instead of considering ourselves a peer with ancient man, in the field of imagination, we have taken the position of a subordinate, and adopted his contracted and erroneous views of the great plan of life.

As a profession we are indulging in a glory of intellectual attainment, and the world of thought has been made to believe that our present mental emotions arise from unquestioned premises; we are sailing over the sea of time, reveling in the sunshine of worldly fame, which contributes to our pride and bestows its applause of honor. Our department of learning is so skillfully entrenched and baricaded that no other department can attack our citadel of wisdom with any assurance of success; we have the ability to perpetuate our errors for another century to come, and feel that our premises are impregnable to any assault, except from those of our own profession. It becomes us then to consider whether we will break away from the moorings to which tradition has bound us, and strive to recover the harmonious plan ordained for the manifestations of human life; or continue in pursuit of that phantom imagination, which has no prototype in the plans of the Deity.

THE DRIFT OF MEDICAL RESEARCH AND ITS INFLUENCE ON THE PEOPLE.

There is a confessed inability to solve multitudes of medical problems, on a plan of relative harmony; or even to maintain a code of principles, which by analogy affords us a hopeful future; and among the various adopted principles for the establishment of the science, there is scarcely a doubt relative to the correctness of those in use.

The great desideratum according to this belief, is, that a more profound exploration in the present direction will eventually unearth something which will illuminate the shady corners of our science, and transmit a brilliancy in the direction of positiveness, on a level with other sciences; consequently there is little or no reconsideration of the premises, or examination of those doctrines which have been adopted with a view to give the imprint of stability to our department; but an implicit and undoubted faith is manifested in the mental ability and correctness of the imagination of those who erected the guide-boards of our science a few hundred years ago. Those chirographic characters have not been examined to see if they give a true expression to the language of nature, but have only been repainted from time to time, to keep alive their conspicuousness; and the index finger points to-day as it did in the days of Acron, who is mentioned by Pliny as the first to apply philosophical reasoning to medicine. We have been traveling for centuries in accordance with the direction of that index finger, but have not got there; we have not mastered the sciences; we have established a very excellent system of practice, but have not acquired the ability to talk about it, except in a practical manner; theory is so unsatisfactory that it is fast drifting into the museum of lost arts. Our knowledge of the laws of nature, as applied to the facts of nature, is so discordant and dissatisfactory, that he who endeavors to explain the facts, by setting forth the laws or theory, is liable to be considered diminutive or visionary in the judgment of medical men.

The astronomer can explain his facts, because the law on which they are predicated in nature is understood; the medical philosopher cannot explain the facts of his department, because nature's laws are not understood. I ask what other department of scientific thought stands on our books in the same attitude as that adopted by the ancients? History informs us that we have had to correct all departments of philosophy except medical; and yet medical science is the most profound science instituted by the hands of the great Architect.

Were the ancients more wise in this department than in others? or must we admit that the time has not arrived which permits of a reconstruction in a satisfactory manner. The prosecution of thought by the profession to-day is not for reconstructive purposes, but for acquiring a greater speed in the direction of that index finger; although different and rival systems of practice have sprung up which may satisfy the ignorant, but science has no rival. There is but one science, but one way of practicing medicine scientifically; and the reason we have made no satisfactory progress in medical philosophy, is not because we are incompetent, but because we are looking in the wrong direction, drifting along with the tide of disconsolate reason, with our observation and belief on the alert for the discovery of a new power in some combination of correlative medical forces, which will not wane or weary in that time of need, when more momentum is required to keep in motion the machinery of life.

An examination of medical literature, in the various journals devoted to the interests of our science, will furnish sufficient proof that the investigating tendency is largely in the direction of new remedies; and we occupy to-day very much the position of the devotee of fashion who is trimmed in accordance with the Parisian style. The pharmacists and manufacturing chemists manufacture their "goods" with a view to meet the acceptable sentiment of the profession, comminuting and preparing in soluble form the various new preparations for the purpose of affording a material which will become both a medicine and a food; being manipulated with extreme care, and of the *choicest chemicals*, whereby the compounds are supposed to be really chemical food, and are thus labeled, highly lauded, and generally used, until practical experience chooses to discard them, and adopt a more modern invention.

Too often, instead of administering a placebo to pacify the mind of a peculiar patient, the reverse is true, and we are the victims of misplaced confidence, and are treated to a mental placebo, in administering some high-priced inoffensive preparation, with the expectation of its powers executing valuable service, while in reality the patient is being cured by the unaided law of his own vital force. There is one redeeming consolation in perpetuating this error of a belief in medical power, which is, that one can speak a great amount of nonsense, and nobody will know it, and it is really taken for wisdom.

It is not to be questioned that this great error of our time, of incorrect thought, has largely influenced our habits in life, and that we are freighted with untold miseries which a more correct interpretation would have obliterated a century ago; thus as a people we are suffering in body for the mental errors committed by our forefathers. Instead of being in possession of the acquired knowledge of the law which enables life to be most advantageously manifested, we are the victims of inherited beliefs which have long neglected, and ever been slow to establish the sanitary surroundings which favor the longevity of our own race.

For all our shortcomings in bodily health, we have been educated to depend largely, very largely, on a transmuted power to afford relief; and instead of being taught to economize and husband our vital resources, we have been permitted to waste our energies with the belief that other energies could be substituted therefor.

We have become a nation of medicine-takers, and the great and overwhelming idea possessed by the people is that the chief duty of a physician consists in administering foreign active powers to the human organism, to execute the actions of life.

In proof of this firmly implanted idea, we have only to look to the field of quackery and patent nostrum vending, so generously supported and encouraged by our people. This belief is not only sapping the vitality of our nation, but is a draft on their purses a thousand times greater than is levied by our government. This belief inspires an unquestioned confidence, which places the most ignorant pretender and bombast on a level with educated physicians, and detracts ruinously from the reputed superiority of a professional education, and is the unavoidable sequence of our committed error. This may seem severe on the disciples of our science, yet it is the truth, and must be known in order to be corrected.

In order to correct the habits of the people it is not necessary to make medical experts of them, but to give them the right direction, and thus, to illustrate, the science of astronomy is no better understood by the non-professional than is the science of medicine, although the people have been taught that the laws must be understood by which computations and calculations are correctly made, otherwise all predictions would be futile. The people have learned to regard as an impostor any one whose garb and language implied ignorance of the laws which move planetary bodies, whatever might be his pretensions.

It is not so with medical science. We have not educated the people that to be correct physicians it was necessary to understand the vital law, but have waived most of these pretensions, and are inculcating the idea that a knowledge of the *power* which medicines possess enables the physician to supply the required energies for continuing the functions of life.

With this understanding of the premises, is it strange that the people are so easily influenced by quacks and pretenders? Is it strange that this strong faith in such powers should make diminutive the importance of whose hands it came through? Is it strange that this seemingly great required want of varied and increased powers, which we are taught can be supplied by medicine, should occasion to be bottled and pilled, and kept for sale like bread and meat, those powers for the people to purchase at their liking, without the aid of the middle man, physician?

Certainly not; such are the legitimate sequences of a science which is not self-supporting, which cannot give safe direction to the habits of the people, and whose principles remain enshrouded in mystery.

It may be humiliating to our pride to be thus confronted, but if there was any mild gentle persuasive manner, that would dispossess the profession of this great error, I would gladly adopt it.

We are to teach the people, that the science of medicine is based on a knowledge of but one law: namely, the law of vital power; that medicine cannot be used scientifically and safely, without a knowledge of how this vital force behaves in health and disease; a knowledge whether this vital force is doing the best for our welfare which the case permits, and requires only to be let alone and watched, or whether it requires to be medicated; and also how this vital force behaves in relation to the various kinds of medicine.

Then, and not until then, will the science of medicine assume the position where it belongs. When the people are made to believe and understand the importance of these premises, quacking and patent medicine patronage will fail to encourage that faith which now permits human life to be trusted in the hands of an ignoramus. Then will the traffickers in inveigled medical powers become as insignificant as one would to-day in pretending to sell the power or force of chemical affinity, or the power of gravitation.

Another misery entailed on humanity, in consequence of the belief of a power in medicine, is *intemperance*, which is largely augmented by the belief that alcoholic stimulus imparts a power to the human organism.

Alcoholic stimulus is a valuable article of Materia Medica, when properly used, to occasion a changed or increased vital action in certain directions, more favorable to the maintenance of life; but the knowledge which enables it to be used and not abused is not found in the universal application which supposes that any man is wise enough to prescribe for himself.

Through this education of thus receiving accessions of power, and the peculiar sensation of happiness, by its nervine effect, many have been induced to continue its use until the habit, with its miseries, becomes developed beyond the power of good resolution to restore. The power of moral suasion is of inestimable value and yet has been overrated in its expected applicability to the race; and it is in the lesson we are about to learn that the errors and miseries growing out of mistaken science are responsible for a state of society which moral suasion has endeavored to correct. The forces of moral suasion have been rallied and its energies spent, and yet the enemy scarcely disturbed in its slumber. I trust the reader can see what the temperance reform is contending with; one school of instructors educate the people in a manner which largely tends to form bad habits. The other school of instruction is endeavoring to suppress the habits which a previous education incurs, because those habits entail misery.

Science should so provide for our future that education would not conflict with moral suasion and law; so long as education conflicts with legislation, legal enactments will continue to be unpopular and of little avail.

A community of intelligent humanity would be controlled by education and moral suasion even if there was no law; the enactment of certain statutes are to control that class of people who are not susceptible to moral and intellectual forces, either from inability or selfishness.

The large majority of our people who give approved and practical support to our laws, are those who judge of the merits of a law, by their previous education. Therefore, it is self-evident that no law can receive proper and popular support against the convictions of our indoctrinated, erroneous principles. Correct education, moral suasion, and proper law go hand in hand, and are not opposing influences; what the people and the temperance question first require is more education, instead of more law.

CONCLUSION.

THE satisfactory study of a science should embrace a diligent inquiry into all of its fundamental principles; interpret them correctly, and thus establish the premises for an examination of all sides of a question in such a manner as to corroborate the correctness of a conclusion. The memory of spoken words does not constitute the recovery of the principle of medical philosophy, but the mental recognition of the principle becomes essential, that the student may express the principle in his own language. The ideas of Medical Science grow too much out of customs of speech, instead of primary principles, Science, from the hand of its maker, is instituted on fundamental premises as harmonious as the magnetic needle, always pointing in the same direction, and the discord in its unlike representations, is due to a lack of mental perception, in recovering the true significance of nature's language in her efforts to express her principles. Professor Tyndall expressed the following idea in a recent lecture in Boston: "There are three great theories which enable the human mind to open the secrets of nature — the theory of gravitation, the mechanical theory of heat, and the undulatory theory of light. These three pillars, as far as human intellect is concerned, support the universe." Tyndall should include the theory of vitality, which explains the relative position and laws of the vegetable and animal kingdoms. For when we acquire sufficient comprehension to drink in those principles which "support the universe," it certainly should include the vegetable and animal creations, which are no small part of that executive duty perfected through the agency of ordained law.

Tyndall's three theories do not include the human race.

Mankind has long overlooked the idea that vitality was a special principle in nature, governed by its own laws, and consequently we have long been endeavoring to account for what vital force was doing, through the agency of supposed special principles inherent to a low order of creation outside the domains of life.

THE PLAN OF HUMAN LIFE.

We have a nervous system, which fulfills for us those duties which are fulfilled similarly in organizations low in the scale of animal life. That is, there is an instinctive organic force generated in accordance with the creative ability of nerve ganglionic centers, completely outside of the will, which is possessed of a distinguishing selective ability of appropriating and assimilating what becomes necessary for the individual maintenance, and eschewing that which is hurtful or non-usable.

These are implanted principles for self-preservation, without which we could hardly live a day. One distinguishing principle between animal organic life and the organic life of vegetation, consists in the latter having the ability to absorb only what is beneficial, with no power of elimination, not even of its own waste matter, but it must store it up within the organization; while the animal organism absorbs both usable and unusable material, with a power to eliminate its own effete material, and limited ability to eliminate foreign material.

Thus animal organic life is endowed with a self-preservative power, and the individual organism is developed and defended by a generated force, through the ganglionic centers, called instinct. How instinct generates power is an inquiry which extends beyond and anterior to philosophical research; we shall never know how it is generated any more than we shall know how the power of gravitation is generated. It is within our limits only to seize it as it is, and study its manifestations through its different properties of organic perception and action.

Instinct has but two properties, namely, perception by contact or sensation, and contractility or the ability to execute motion; these constitute its two ultimate vital properties.

Instinct, throughout all animal life, from the lowest animal organism without a brain, to the highest man with a cerebrum, is on the same plan, although the degrees of sensations are variable, and the ability to execute motion is developed on a progressive scale. The duty of the instinct is to superintend the building of the organism, to use that material which is proper to be used, and reject that material which is impossible to use, which is known to the instinct through the nerve or vital property called sensation.

Thus the physiological law is the law of the instinctive vital action, in relation to how it uses nutrient material;

and the pathological law is the law of the instinctive vital action in relation to material which is non-usable; therefore, health is the normal action directed by instinct in relation to nutrient material, and disease is the abnormal action directed by instinct in relation to non-nutrient material; consequently the plan of life involves but one ordained power which gives involuntary motion to living tissues.

Thus, as a living human organism, we do not maintain an individuality in relation to the outside or material world, which may be moved, propelled, or acted upon by a multiplicity of inferiorly ordained and imaginative powers; but we are the product of a superior ordained force, and like the planetary system which executes varied phenomena through the realms of space in conformity to the special ordained force or power of gravitation, we as individual organizations execute the functions of life, both voluntary and involuntary, in accordance with a special ordained power. Our activity under all circumstances, in health and disease, is due to an inherent life principle, which recognizes each individual relation to the material world; each individual identity is manifested through the special vital properties sensation, sensibility, and motion, and the organic wants, or likes and dislikes, are practically executed by involuntary motion or activities, generated by the impulse of instinct, which is informed of all presence by sensation. Our individual wants, or likes and dislikes, are practically executed by activities generated by the impulse of the will, or the voluntary powers of brain sensibility.

In the order of development, as the nerve structure becomes more highly endowed, we find superadded to the organic instincts, a higher order of controlling power, usually denominated animal instinct, as applied to that class of animals who build their habitations always on the same plan, and execute certain acts perfectly at birth, as the wasp, beaver, and the chicken that scratches in search of nutriment.

Such endowments are not organic instinct, but are more properly voluntary instincts or semi-brain powers, which give direction to voluntary motion. Voluntary instincts or semi-brain powers have, in fulfillment of duty, the protection of the body after it is organized, while organic instincts arrange the material during the process of organization.

These duties are so unlike, in the kind of labor executed, that the principles of science demand that the term "instinct," unqualified, shall not be applied to both.

The brain power or force is a superadded ability, dependent for its manifestation on a previous fulfillment of organic growth, through the controlling force of instinct; therefore, it is very evident that the lower orders of life can execute their functions, generation after generation, without the aid of the higher endowments; but the higher orders cannot exist without the previous development of the lower. Man is organically that highly elaborated production of the instinctive controlling power, executed on the same plan of primitive principles of animal creation, but more highly endowed with more massive nervous structure, enlarging into a brain. Whatever development we possess is really due to the labors of the involuntary organic instincts; although we may so modify the surroundings as will permit the increase, or retard the growth of those highly elaborated structures.

Thus the range of duty performed by involuntary powers gives organization to structures, which execute voluntary will powers; and man organically is embodied within that department of labor executed by instinct, with its two vital properties, sensation and motion, developing those structures which permit the manifestations of the superadded vital property of sensibility.

Animals may be what man is defined to be organically; but man is even more than what he is organically; he is distinguished functionally, above animal life, with the superadded ability of a greater expanse of the intellect and with the higher qualities of mind, expressed through hope, consciousness, and spirituality. Man, unlike any other organization, is endowed with the ability to know himself; that is, through his sensibility he may look back and survey the premises, or orders of creation beneath him, and compare them with his own. He may behold the silent activity of that law which makes him the possessor of his special endowment, sensibility. He may comprehend the law of that force or instinctive power which both maintains and defends him. Through the sensibility, we have a limited power of correcting those actions of our involuntary life, unlike any other creature.

The beasts of the field and the forest are organized on that plan, which occasions them to partake only of those kinds of food, or swallow little material, except that which the organic instincts may use for constructive purposes; while man, with greater abilities, necessarily has greater responsibilities; his abilities are not only greater in accumulation, but greater in defence; therefore, should he take into his system that material unfit for constructive purposes, he not only has more ability, through the powers of his organic instinct, but his brain powers may comprehend, and direct to a certain extent, these involuntary powers of instinct, in accomplishing their designed duty.

The order of creation, made known to us through the various modes of research, gives ample testimony that there have been periods of life on earth when the highest organization was not equal to our domesticated animals, and that in the human race are combined the results of a successive unfolding of higher and more complicated structural organizations. The various additional developments which have been unfolded through the successive productions of animal life, from the lowest to the highest, do not seem to be a superadded ability to a lower animal, which makes that one a higher animal in the scale of progression, but the specific law of unfolding has its limits in the particular kind, so far as general bodily conformation is concerned, and the special ordained force which forms each organization is unlike all others, in this particular respect, that each ordained force is ushered into activity with a certain definite limit to its unfolding or developmental forms, and that each created organization is the result of a specific, separate ordained force. The premises which particularly warrant this interpretation, in brief, may be found in the evidences of the immutability of God's plans. It would be a dangerous precedent to accept His ways as being changeable.

We are all, as distinguished in the separate animal races, the special result of a separate ordained force; although our attainments are not special providences, but the result of conformity and strict adherence to the special law of force; whereby we receive the greatest blessing ordained for us, thus making us accountable beings, — accountable for the fulfillment of the conditions which enable us to reap the rewards provided for our welfare.

Certain definite proportions are conformed to in the creation of the various kinds of animal life, which not only gives expression to their individuality, but gives an ability for self-defence; which conformity becomes essential for voluntary animal functions; thus the long-legged animal rapidly measures distance between himself and the enemy, while the more ferocious fight it out on the spot.

Throughout the domain of animal life shape gives an index to the peculiar character and ability of the organizations; and this law holds good even in mankind. There must be a limit, however, to the general principle involved in the construction of bodily forms; and we have many reasons for accepting the human form as the nearest perfect for the development of the brain abilities.

Therefore, so far as the plan of general bodily form is involved, nature has fulfilled the extreme of her ordained ability; and the unfolding or higher orders of development are no longer in the direction of bodily shape, but the direction of the particular organ, brain.

The unfoldings of nature, during the age of men, are in relation to the increased capabilities of brain force. Our ordained abilities in this direction are not fulfilled, our capabilities are not circumscribed; a few great minds have shot far ahead of the majority; but the end is not yet. Not only have we an intellectual range to develop, but there are also almost unknown brain abilities to be developed, quite unlike our general preconceived views. Thus we are not only organized capable of looking backwards, and surveying the mighty results of His Works, but we are endowed with abilities which enable us to look forward toward the future. Brain and intellect are created and manifested by a process of constructive lifting up; thus the brain is directly developed through the actions of other powers, which make the organ. We cannot have intellect without a brain, nor a brain without the constructive fulfillment of instinctive action. Intellect is not the highest attribute manifested through organization, for we have superadded to our intellectual powers certain functions, or rather qualities of a higher nature, hope, conscience, and the soul principle spirituality, which are more than intellect, yet manifested only through the intellect.

We cannot manifest a soul principle without intellect, nor intellect without a brain, nor a brain without a previous aggregation of matter, in accordance with the law of organic instinct, nor a manifestation of animal organic instinct without a previous fulfillment of vegetative organic law; and anterior to this must exist the activity of atomic changes in accordance with the laws of chemistry; the whole to be preceded by Him who creates not only the material, but ordains the law which fulfills all these activities which our sensibility perceives; thus the extremes meet or simulate, the created and the Creator know each other.

God possesses greater power than we always attribute to Him; instead of wielding that influence which we perceive in activity, and often express as His Will, it is His Will indirect; that is, He creates not only the material, but ordains the law which gives activity to this material, which must be obeyed in order to fulfill the objects of His Will, and for aught we know He is a silent observer of His Works.

It is through His Works only that we know Him; likewise with our race: it is not the material man, but the works of mankind, which enable us to know them; which give value, infusing sentiments that continue with the future. God not only creates the material, but He ordains the law, giving to it the imprints of its mission; thus He ordains the force *which is* inseparate and inclusive, that stamps the individuality of our existence, and enables us to be what we ourselves and the generations before us have permitted us to be through them, by conformity or otherwise to those laws which should be known, and conditions supplied that the best results thereby may be fulfilled.

That force which establishes our existence is embodied, that is, in the inclusive sense, with the primary abilities which develop a body, with its manifestations of organic instincts, and develops our brain for the manifestation of intellect; and develops our soul principle for the manifestation of those higher qualities; we have all these in the outstart as a primal gift, to develop our natures in fulfillment of the plan of human accountability.

And what we fall short of or fail to possess, humanity is alone responsible for, either by transgression or omission, along the pathway of past generations or the career of our own present life. With these premises before us, omission is to sin against opportunity or knowledge. Consequently, it becomes our duty to know the laws which develop and maintain our body, that we may improve ourselves by physical culture, which constructs a better and more enduring brain. And the brain should also be cultured, not alone for the degree of intellect which it may be possible to attain, but through it more intelligently to cultivate the moral and religious sentiments, or the soul principle of our nature.

The value of a body, as a body, consists in the total of its instinctive energies harmoniously balanced, or in other words, its power of development and enduring abilities. The value of a brain, as a brain, consists in the total of its intellectual abilities, which benefits the individual and the race, comprehending the most of the universe and those higher qualities which relate us to infinity.

The value of a soul, consists not in the fact that it is a principle of our nature stamped with the imprint of immortality, but in the degree of its religious culture and practical workings in relation to surrounding humanity.

There is a great tendency in the study of material man to gravitate towards the conclusion, that all he is, is the result of organization; that consequently, when that structure, the brain, which manifests both the intellectual and the soul principle, becomes destroyed, he is no more, or, in other words, the material through which he has established an individuality dissolves his existence and makes the future a blank.

It is very rational that man should frequently, and even more frequently than he allows himself to confess, arrive at such a state of contemplation of human destiny, not however because it is true, but because he does not comprehend sufficient of the principles ordained for his development. He is liable to infer that the soul principle is developed *after*, arriving at maturity, instead of being an ever-present special principle, undergoing a slow or rapid development.

Mankind start in life from the hand of the Creator, in possession of those immortal principles which are manifested in the development of the material body and brain, through which one is to express, maintain, and develop his identity and accountability; thus he begins with a starting germ of invisible power or principle, which awaits the law of its own development; for its manifestation to our senses, consequently, along the pathway of life, there is existing that principle which develops the body to its full size, unless human agencies either remote or proximate have intervened; there is the principle which fulfills the possibilities for an intellectual attainment, which will be manifest unless human agencies have curtailed the fulfillment of the design. There is also the soul-principle germ, if I may use the term, awaiting the process of development through other *previous* fulfillments. Thus, at any stage of life, there is an immortal or soul principle, more or less developed, to be returned to its Maker, bringing back the fruits of the mission for which it was started.

This is the only plan on which we can harmonize the philosophy of human life and the doctrines of theology with man's accountability to himself and to God, as a free moral agent.

If man was the product of evolutionary development on the Darwinian theory, his soul principle would be an appendage to organization, rather than a primary principle stamped with the imprint of immortality; and instead of special and primal ordained principles of force which fulfill the mission for which they are established, the forces of creation would have no fixed identity to fulfill in different animal races; and we might as well expect gravitation to turn into some other force, and chemical and vital forces to change their avocations, as to believe that the different animal species fail to fulfill in development the full limit of the ordained design through the special force which perfects this individual existence. Instead of order we should have disorder.

If man's brain was highly endowed without man's efforts, he would not be accountable; if man's soul-principle was created in the fulfillment of its activities, he would require no religious culture, and possess no moral accountability; consequently, along the pathway of life there must be different degrees of intellectual development, and different degrees of soul development, and at premature death with the former, there must be less loss to remaining man, and with the latter less returned to God.

Religious culture does not consist alone in establishing the belief or faith among men that there is an immortal principle within them for which they should continue to express gratitude in formal praise and song, although it embraces those premises which are but a very small part of men's religious duties. The ability to give zest to song or enthusiasm to prayer, may express emotional qualities which have an influence to impress the hearer with a sympathetic intuition of the importance of religious culture, and he feels that he is converted: it is but conversion to belief, not conversion to possessed wisdom; without sufficient wisdom these conversions are liable to merge into transparency.

Thus, unadulterated religion must necessarily be highly seasoned with intelligence in order to be consistent with itself.

In support of the theory that the soul-principle is an ever present part of invisible humanity, which we have already been persuaded to believe, through the instrumentality of faith, is the demonstration from those devout exercises in which heathen men participate with implicit faith, although undeveloped intellect.

Belief is not religion, although it may influence us to cultivate and manifest religion. A strong belief in the divine wisdom of God and the mission of Christ, with a weak intellect or undeveloped mentality, makes persons seem to be hypocrites, although they may not be so any more than the heathen, for they act up to their intelligence. A strong belief in the importance of a great intellect without possessing it, does not make the believer equal to the one who does possess it; nor the firm belief in the importance of religion without the intellectual ability to execute it, or even if neglected in its active fulfillment, does not make that religious believer equal to a Christian.

It is a religious duty to develop and maintain bodily

health, also to cultivate the intellect, for it is only through the two that we are enabled to manifest that religious element which cannot be otherwise cultivated. Intentions may be good, and the heathen may sacrifice human life to propitiate the anger of the gods; therefore, if the comprehension is not what it should be, we do not fulfill uprightly those practical duties which alone constitute religious conduct. The zealous believer with small brain capabilities is very liable to be so in love with God's will and way, that he often attempts to render service to God by assisting Him in the punishment of mankind.

When we praise God it becomes us to inquire of ourselves whether we praise Him through the convictions of our perceptive wisdom and appreciation of His greatness, or whether we do it parrot like, with a language which has but little intellect or soul in it.

The doctrine of repentance is sometimes erroneously taught; our souls are not lost without repentance; that is, whatever there may be of this principle developed, which is always more or less, and which is returned to God; but without repentance and correct ways of life we lose what we should otherwise acquire, or fail to save that which it was ordained that we should develop in order to be acceptable.

I have previously said that the present unfolding of God's powers were not in relation to bodily form, but in relation to the development of the brain. A comparison of the Christian brain with the heathen is in proof of this order of progression, and that we are yet pursuing the progressing tendency, but are a long distance from its maximum glory.

The expanse of the intellect and the soul must go hand in hand; it cannot be otherwise; but intellectual ambition is too easily satisfied, and the doctrines of theology sometimes tend to contract the intellect, in its endeavors to expand the faith. Faith without intellect makes a heathen; with it, makes the Christian. Religious faith, without proper intellect, is selfish, and strives to guard its supposed premises against the development of science, as if science was an enemy to religion. Everything which is called religion may not be religion, everything which is called science may not be science.

True science, instead of conflicting with true religion, supports and substantiates it; the religion of this age takes its advanced position through the better understanding of God's law, which is science; what theology cannot do to Christianize the world, science can; when theology staggers at its task, science comes to the rescue.

www.ingramcontent.com/pod-product-compliance
Lightning Source LLC
Chambersburg PA
CBHW030347170426
43202CB00010B/1285